# ESSENTIALS OF MARKETING

Editors:

MC Cant

JW Strydom

CJ Jooste

Authors:

A Brink

JA Bennet

R Machado

**JUTA**

First published 1999


©Juta & Co Ltd
PO Box 14373, Kenwyn, 7790

ISBN 0 7021 5203X


Sub-editing: Pinpoint Publishing Services cc, Johannesburg
Cover design: Linda Lurie, Cape Town

Typesetting: B J Schwartz, Johannesburg

Printed and bound by Creda Communications
Eliot Avenue, Eppindust II, Cape Town, South Africa

# PREFACE

Essentials of marketing is designed to give students the opportunity to learn about marketing in an enjoyable and practical way. Marketing takes place all around us. Marketing is an essential service in all types of businesses, from manufacturing companies to wholesalers and retailers to service organisations. It is fair to say that marketing is essential to all kinds of individuals and organisations. You will realise how widespread marketing is when it emerges that large retailers, doctors, lawyers, dentists, politicians and even churches use marketing techniques all the time.

It is therefore important that these organisations know what marketing is, what the marketing environment entails, how to research the market properly, which factors influence consumers' behaviour and how to segment the market.

All these tasks are performed in order to satisfy the needs of the customers and to eventually influence a decision on what specific product(s) to offer, at what price, where the products should be offered and how the customers should be informed of the products.

Essentials of marketing has been designed as a result of the developments in higher education. The current trend is towards the modular system of teaching as well as a focus on specialist degrees and diplomas. Essentials of marketing has been structured to provide student marketers with a good foundation for the formulation of a marketing strategy. We believe that this book serves this purpose and that it is ideally suited for a modular course in marketing. The authors of the text are all specialists in their fields. The fact that the authors are all experienced writers of professional articles and academic texts and have read many papers at international conferences as well as have vast practical experience, ensures that this text achieves a good balance between the academic and practical approaches to marketing.

Care has been taken to present the content in a logical and systematic manner and this text has succeeded in achieving this.

The following authors have been involved in the writing of this text:

* Chapter 1 - Prof Michael Cant (Unisa).
* Chapter 2 - Prof Johan Strydom (Unisa).
* Chapter 3 - Dr Annekie Brink (Unisa).
* Chapter 4 - Prof Alf Bennet (RAU).
* Chapter 5 - Prof Chris Jooste (RAU).
* Chapter 6 - Mr Ricardo Machado (Unisa).


We trust that you will enjoy using Essentials of marketing and that you will benefit from the content.


MC CANT
JW STRYDOM
CJ JOOSTE
November 1999

# CONTENTS

# CHAPTER 1

## THE MARKETING WORLD

## 1.1 INTRODUCTION[1]

The main objectives of most businesses are survival, profits, and growth and marketing contributes directly to achieving these objectives. Marketing includes the following activities:

- assessing the wants and needs of current and future customers;

- developing and managing product offerings;

- determining prices and pricing policies;

- developing distribution strategies; and

- communicating with current and future customers.

Marketing plays a major role in our everyday life. We participate in the marketing process as consumers of products and services. About half of every rand spent pays for marketing costs, which includes marketing research, product development, packaging, transportation, storage, advertising, and sales expenses. By developing a better understanding of marketing, you will become a better-informed consumer. You will better understand the buying process and be able to negotiate more effectively with sellers. Moreover, you will be better prepared to demand satisfaction when the products and services you buy do not meet the standards promised by the manufacturer or the marketer.

The main aim of all marketing activity is to facilitate *mutually satisfying exchanges between parties*. The activities of marketing include the *conception*, *pricing*, *promotion* and *distribution* of ideas, products and services.

The role of marketing and the character of marketing activities within a business are strongly influenced by its philosophy and orientation. A *production-oriented* business focuses on the internal capabilities of the company rather than on the desires and needs of the marketplace.

A *sales orientation* is based on the beliefs that people will buy more products if aggressive sales techniques are used and that high sales volumes produce high profits.

A *marketing-oriented* business focuses on satisfying customer wants and needs while meeting company objectives. A *societal marketing orientation* goes beyond a pure marketing orientation to include the preservation or enhancement of individuals' and society's long-term best interests.

To implement the marketing concept successfully, management must enthusiastically embrace and endorse the concept and encourage its spread throughout the business. Changing from a production or sales orientation to a marketing orientation often requires changes in management authority and responsibility.

The marketing process includes:

■ understanding the business's mission and the role marketing plays in fulfilling that mission;

■ setting marketing objectives;

■ scanning the environment;

■ developing a marketing strategy by selecting a target market strategy;

■ developing and implementing a marketing mix;

■ implementing the marketing strategy;

■ designing performance measures; and

■ evaluating marketing efforts and making changes, if needed.

The marketing mix combines *product*, *distribution (place)*, *marketing communication* and *pricing* strategies in a way that creates exchanges satisfying to individual and company objectives. All these aspects are discussed in this chapter.

---

### LEARNING OUTCOMES

At the end of this chapter you will be able to:

■ explain what marketing is;

■ explain the concept of exchange;

■ explain the marketing activities;

■ discuss the orientations towards marketing;

---

- define marketing;

- explain the marketing process; and

- discuss the marketing function in the business.

## 1.2 THE NATURE OF MARKETING

### 1.2.1 What is marketing?[2]

The term 'marketing' means many things to many people. Some people think it means personal selling, while others consider marketing to be the same as advertising. Others believe that marketing means making products available in shops, arranging displays and maintaining inventories of products for future sales. In reality, marketing includes all of these activities, and more.

Marketing has two facets. Firstly, it is a philosophy, an attitude, a perspective, or a management orientation that stresses customer satisfaction. Secondly, marketing is the range of activities used to implement such a philosophy. The American Marketing Association's definition encompasses both perspectives:

'Marketing is the process of planning and executing the conception, pricing, marketing communication and distribution of ideas, products, and services to create exchanges that satisfy individual and organisational goals.'

The activities listed in the definition refer to specific decision-making areas of marketing management.

Today, marketing must be understood not in the old sense of making a sale but in the new sense of satisfying customer needs. If the marketer does a good job of understanding consumer needs, develops products that offer value, and prices, distributes and promotes them effectively, the products will sell.

Everyone knows something about 'hot' (or 'cool' ) products. When Kreepy Krawly designed its first automatic pool cleaner, the manufacturer was swamped with orders. They had designed the 'right' product: not 'me-too' products, but a new one offering new benefits.

## 1.2.2 The concept of exchange

**Exchange** is the key term in the marketing process. The **concept of exchange** is quite simple. It means that people give up something to receive something they would rather have. Normally, we think of money as the medium of exchange. We 'give up' money to 'get' the products and services we want. Exchange does not necessarily require money, however[3]. Items and services may be bartered or traded: house-sitting for free accommodation; fresh produce for manufactured goods.

For any kind of exchange to take place, five conditions must prevail[4]:

1.  There must be at least two parties.

2.  Each party must have something that the other party values.

3.  Each party must be able to communicate with the other party and deliver the goods or services sought by the other.

4.  Each party must be free to accept or reject the other's offer.

5.  Each party must want to deal with the other party.

These conditions prevail in what is commonly referred to as a **market**. Exchange will not necessarily take place even when all these conditions exist. They are, however, necessary for exchange to be possible. For example, you may place an advertisement in a newspaper stating that your used car is for sale at a certain price. Several people may call you to ask about it, some may look at it, and one or more may even make you an offer. But unless you reach an agreement with a buyer and actually sell the car, an exchange will not take place[5].

## 1.2.3 Gaps between production and consumption

In the modern business environment, the place where a product is produced is not necessarily the place where it is consumed. This means that 'gaps' exist between production and consumption, which can be identified by considering some **core marketing aspects**.

Figure 1.1 shows that the core marketing aspects are linked, with each aspect building on the one before it.

Bearing in mind the principles illustrated in Figure 1.1, consider the situation of a consumer who needs a small quantity of milk. She must be able to obtain a specific package size, from an outlet close to where she lives, and she must have the medium of exchange – money – to enable the exchange to take place.

Possible gaps include the convenience of access to the outlet, transport of the product in saleable condition and availability in small sizes, availability of finance, and so on.

## FIGURE 1.1 CORE MARKETING ASPECTS

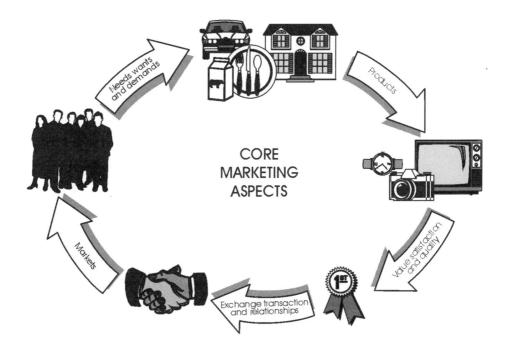

Source: Kotler, P and Armstrong, G. 1996. *Principles of marketing*. 7th edition. Englewood Cliffs, NJ: Prentice Hall, p 6.

According to McInnis[6], five types of gaps can be identified. A proper market offering and successful marketing are possible only if these five gaps have been effectively bridged.

1. **Space gap.** South African Breweries produces Castle Lager mainly in one centre, but beer drinkers are spread throughout southern Africa, leaving a geographical space (distance) between the manufacturer and the consumer.

2. **Time gap.** Mealies are harvested in North West province in winter, but consumers want their mealie meal porridge throughout the year.

3. **Information gap.** A first-time, uninformed computer buyer may not have enough knowledge to make an appropriate purchase.

4. **Ownership gap.** When a new car is purchased, the consumer becomes the owner only when it is registered in his or her name, and this happens only once the car has been paid for.

5. **Value gap.** Seller and buyer must agree on an acceptable exchange rate (price of the product). If buyers perceive a price to be unacceptably high, they will not buy; if sellers cannot get the price they want, they will not offer to sell. The value the buyer attaches to the product should ideally be the same as that attached by the seller.

## 1.2.4 Needs, wants and demands

**Needs, wants and demands** of people are complex. Needs refer to basic physical needs, such as for food, clothing and safety. Social needs refer to a need to belong to a group, and for affection. Unmet or unsatisfied needs compel people to try and reduce the need or to look for something that will satisfy it.

Wants are the form taken by human needs as they are shaped by culture and an individual's personality. Wants are described in terms of objects that will satisfy needs.

When backed by buying power, wants become demands. A marketing-oriented company will do much to learn about and understand their customers' needs, wants and demands.

**Products** are what people use to satisfy their needs and wants. A product can be defined as anything offered to a market to satisfy people's/customers' needs or wants. Products can be either tangible, such as a car, or intangible (service), such as consulting services.

**Value** can be defined as the difference between the value the customer gains from owning and using a product and the costs of obtaining the product. **Satisfaction**, on the other hand, depends on a products' perceived performance in delivering value relative to a buyer's expectations. **Customer satisfaction** is closely linked to quality, as quality has a direct impact on product performance, and therefore on customer satisfaction.

Businesses offer their products to customers, who perceive it as offering value for money and that it will satisfy their needs. Customers then engage in a **transaction** to obtain the product or service. **Exchange** therefore takes place. If the exchange leads to mutual satisfaction, the basis is laid for creating a **relationship** between the parties.

The concept of exchange leads to the concept of a **market**. A market consists of **buyers** and **sellers** of a product, and both offer something of value – the seller offers a product/service and the buyer offers money/labour.

## 1.2.5 Intermediaries

As trade and business practices evolved over time, the distance (literally and figuratively) between buyer and seller increased. The need for an acceptable medium of exchange which symbolised the value (or price) of exchanged products resulted in the development of a monetary system. This enabled participants to exchange products not for other products of equal value but rather for the acceptable medium of exchange (gold coins or other forms of payment).

The transporting of products from producer to consumer and the conveying of information also became increasingly complicated, creating an opportunity for the specialised services of *intermediaries*, operating as go-betweens for the participants in the exchange, who were no longer in close contact. The first intermediaries were probably travelling hawkers who traded in a variety of products and also conveyed vital information about potential markets and desirable new products. They earned income for their trouble by selling to consumers at a higher price than they had paid to the producer. The participants in these activities were as follows:

> SELLER – INTERMEDIARY – BUYER.

In today's business environment there are mainly three kinds of intermediaries:

1. **Middlemen** are enterprises directly involved in taking title, or ownership, of products, which are later sold to others. Pick 'n Pay is a middleman for the redistribution of many different products, bought from hundreds of producers and offered to thousands of customers, under the same roof.

2. **Sales intermediaries** are agents who do not take title of products they sell. They provide services to facilitate the sales process and are paid for these services.

3. **Auxiliary enterprises** are not directly involved in the transfer of title but provide support services to facilitate the selling process. Examples are Spoornet, advertising agencies, and commercial banks.

In today's society, the desire for new and enjoyable things plays a crucial role in economic development. Without this desire, stagnation and decline are inevitable. Today there are few situations where actual bartering is used as a method of satisfying human needs. Exchange media such as paper money and credit cards were developed and hawkers made way for large wholesalers and retailers to facilitate exchanges between buyers and sellers. Communication media such as the press, radio and television helped to spread information on the availability of competing products. Because of these developments, services gained in importance.

These days, there are many specialists offering desirable services instead of products. The basis for marketing, as we experience it today, has been laid. There is a big market consisting of people with a wide variety of needs which create a demand for all kinds of need-satisfying products and services. Sellers try to fulfil these needs in order to satisfy their own. There are also many different sellers competing and obviously this leads to the development of a variety of new, improved products. Buyers need to make a suitable selection from this variety because they usually have only limited means. The need-satisfying and real intrinsic value of different products is therefore carefully considered by buyers and weighed against the exchange medium which must be sacrificed to obtain the product. The price of a specific product reflects the value of that product to the buyer. Today a buyer does not merely buy a physical object, he or she buys a market offering which combines the physical object with other need-satisfying qualities.

The market offering consists of a *product* with a recognisable name, available at a convenient *place*, at a *price* which truly reflects its value for the buyer.

## 1.3  MARKETING ACTIVITIES

The different marketing activities involved in the transfer of a market offering to buyers has briefly been mentioned. The following *primary, auxiliary* and *exchange* activities can now be distinguished.[7]

The *primary* marketing activity is transport. From donkeys and camels, transport methods have developed to pipelines, land, water and air traffic, each with its own unique advantages and disadvantages. The purpose of these forms of transport is to deliver the product to the consumer in the quickest and safest way.

Auxiliary marketing activities are the following:

- **Obtaining and supplying information.** The seller must know who and where potential buyers are. He or she can find this out by conducting marketing research. Thereafter, he or she can supply information to potential buyers by using marketing communication methods such as advertising and personal selling.

- **Standardisation and grading.** Manufactured products must be designed to conform to specific norms or standards. Agricultural products are graded according to certain qualities. Eggs, for example, are graded according to size. This facilitates the buying process, making it easier for the buyer to buy.

- **Storage.** This is an activity that can close the time gap. Seasonal production of agricultural products necessitates storage to ensure the ready availability of these products throughout the year. Warehouses are normally used for storage. For example, mealies are stored in silos from where they are delivered to milling companies as needed for distribution to wholesalers and retailers.

- **Financing.** Costs are incurred in the transfer of products and services from sellers to buyers. These costs must be financed, usually by banks and other financial institutions. All participants in the exchange process should strive to keep financing costs down to present the product at a price acceptable to the consumer and worthwhile to the seller.

- **Risk-taking.** The owner of the product is exposed to the risk of loss or damage and can insure the goods against some risks, such as arson, theft and storm damage.

**Exchange** marketing activities are **buying** and **selling**. Ownership is transferred from one party to another. Buying activities are not regarded as a marketing task but rather as the responsibility of a business's purchasing department. Selling, on the other hand, is a very important task of the marketing department of a business. These marketing activities have been influenced by the orientation towards markets which prevailed at the time.

## 1.4 ORIENTATION TOWARDS MARKETS[8]

Four competing orientations have strongly influenced business's marketing activities over the years. These orientations are commonly referred to as **production, sales,** pure **marketing,** and **societal marketing** orientations. Each of these is now discussed.

## 1.4.1 Production orientation

A production orientation focuses on the ***internal capabilities*** of the business rather than on the desires and needs of the marketplace. A ***production orientation*** means that management assesses its resources and asks questions such as 'What can we do best?'; 'What can our engineers design?'; 'What is easy to produce, given our equipment?'. In the case of a service organisation, managers ask 'What services are most convenient for the business to offer?' and 'Where do our talents lie?'[9]

A production orientation's major shortfall lies in the fact that it does not consider whether the goods and services that the business produces most efficiently also meet the needs of the marketplace. A production orientation does not necessarily doom a company to failure, particularly not in the short run. Sometimes, what a company can best produce is exactly what the market wants. In other situations, for example, when competition is weak or demand exceeds supply, a production-orientation company can survive and even prosper. The long-term fit between what the business manufactures and what the consumer wants is, however, unreliable.

## 1.4.2 Sales orientation[10]

A ***sales orientation*** is based on the premise that people will buy more products and services if aggressive sales techniques are used and that high sales result in high profits. Not only are sales to the final buyer emphasised but ***intermediaries*** are also encouraged to push (promote) a manufacturer's products more aggressively. To sales-oriented businesses, marketing means selling.

The major shortcoming of a sales orientation is a lack of understanding of the needs and wants of the marketplace. Sales-oriented companies often find that, despite the quality of their products and their salesforce, they cannot convince people to buy products or services that are neither wanted nor needed[11].

### SALES ARE EVERYTHING

There are still many business today operating in the sales-oriented phase, where management is convinced that all marketing problems can be solved by marketing communication only. The importance of the other three marketing instruments is disregarded.

- Management of some mail order businesses is still sales-oriented. These businesses advertise products that in fact are not readily available or not worth the price quoted. Advertisements promise all kinds of unrealistic benefits. In an effort to stop such unethical sales practices, responsible mail order businesses with long-term objectives in mind are members of an association (Direct Marketers) which keeps a close watch on standards. Consumers can therefore patronise such enterprises with a greater degree of confidence.

- Door-to-door sales have acquired a bad reputation because some salespeople do not allow consumers enough time to make responsible decisions. These salespeople, who are sometimes very good communicators, can easily persuade customers to make hasty decisions. After the order has been signed, it is regarded as a contract and the customer is compelled to pay, even if it is to his/her own detriment. To avoid this, a 'cooling down' period is included in some contracts (for example, buying a house). During this period (for example, two days) the customer can cancel the contract if he or she so wishes.

### 1.4.3 Marketing orientation (pure marketing concept)

It was only after the Second World War that a change in management's approach to the market occurred. The production plants producing war material could now be used to satisfy the demand for all sorts of consumer products. Because of the widening gap between the producer and the consumer, management needed reliable information on how best to satisfy consumer needs. A change from sales-oriented management to marketing-oriented management resulted in an emphasis not only on the **sales message** and the **price** but also on the **quality** of products, **packaging, methods of distribution** and the necessity of **providing information** by means of advertising. Consumers also developed more sophisticated needs and were financially in a better position to satisfy these needs. There was a large variety of competing products from which they could choose. This led management to realise the importance of the marketing function. Production could begin only after management obtained market information on what consumers wanted, how much they were willing to pay, and how they could best be reached by means of **advertisements, sales promotion methods, publicity** and **personal selling**.

A *marketing orientation,* which is the foundation of contemporary marketing philosophy, is based on an understanding that a sale depends not on an aggressive salesforce but rather on a customer's decision to purchase a product. What a business thinks it produces is not of primary importance to its success. Instead, what a customer thinks he or she is buying – *the perceived value* – defines a business. Perceived value also determines a business's products and its potential to prosper. To marketing-oriented firms, marketing means building *long-term relationships* with customers[12].

This orientation has led to what is commonly called the *pure marketing concept.*[13] The marketing concept can be regarded as an ethical code or philosophy according to which the marketing task is performed. Many writers agree that the marketing concept serves as a guideline for management decision making. Pride and Ferrell view the marketing concept as '... a way of thinking ... about an organisation's entire activities'.

The essence of the marketing concept lies in three principles:[14]

1. Long-term maximisation of profitability.
2. Consumer orientation.
3. The integration of all business activities directed at profitability and the satisfaction of consumer needs, demands and preferences.

The so-called 'pure marketing concept', consisting of these three basic principles, was severely criticised as being short-sighted because it disregarded environmental changes and problems and focused more on short-term consumer satisfaction rather than on the long-term well-being of society.

## THE OBJECTION AGAINST THE PURE MARKETING CONCEPT

Kotler and Armstrong clearly state the following objection against the pure marketing concept:

'It asks if the firm that senses, serves and satisfies individual wants is always doing what is best for consumers and society in the long run. The pure marketing concept ignores possible conflicts between short-run consumer wants and long-run consumer welfare.'

Source: Kotler, P. and Armstrong, G. 1987. *Marketing: an introduction.* Englewood, Cliffs, NJ: Prentice Hall, p 15

© Juta

It is now appropriate to consider all three principles of the marketing concept in more detail.

## ■ Consumer orientation

Consumer orientation is the first principle of the marketing concept, indicating that all marketing actions should be aimed at satisfying consumer needs, demands and preferences. This, however, does not mean that marketing management must provide for unrealistic consumer needs. The business can provide need satisfaction only in so far as its resources enable it to do so. Achieving the *profitability objective* must also be taken into account in the endeavour to provide for consumer needs. However, failure to appreciate what the consumer wants creates opportunities for competitors and can adversely affect profits.

## ■ Profit orientation

In the free-market system, achieving profitability is of crucial importance. Maximising profitability is the primary objective of a profit-seeking business and can be achieved only with due consideration of consumer needs. This overriding objective is usually expressed in quantitative terms. The business can, for example, strive to attain a *rate of return* on total assets of 25% on investment, and can regard this figure as the maximum profitability which could be achieved in a specific time and under specific conditions.

Profit-seeking enterprises attempt to achieve a specific rate of return on total assets in the long term rather than to obtain unduly high returns in the short term, as a short-term approach can endanger its survival. The long-term nature of the profitability objective distinguishes marketing from the mere bartering transaction from which it originally developed. Various secondary objectives can also be set to facilitate long-term achievement of the primary objective.

Non-profit-seeking organisations focus on effective and efficient utilisation of resources and cost reduction rather than on profits. In an economic decline, a profit-seeking business too can concentrate on efficiency and effectiveness rather than profits in order to protect its position until economic conditions improve and profits can once again be made.

Secondary objectives are set in order to contribute directly or even indirectly to the achievement of the main objective.

### SECONDARY OBJECTIVES

- A secondary objective, for example, can be to enhance the corporate image of the business in the eyes of the public. Achievement of this objective can contribute indirectly to profitability.

- A secondary objective of increasing sales can influence the profit figure directly by increasing the income of the business.

- A secondary objective of promoting awareness of costs in the marketing department can have a direct influence on profit by encouraging cost reduction.

## ■ *Organisational integration*

A system is an integrated whole, a group of related units working together to achieve a joint objective. *Organisational integration* is an important principle of the marketing concept and entails all departments in the business working together to achieve the successful marketing of the business's market offering. All the divisions in the marketing department also direct their activities and decisions towards achieving a specific objective. The four marketing instruments should complement and reinforce one another in such a way that the target market will prefer the business's market offering to that of competitors.

## 1.4.4 Societal marketing orientation[15]

According to the *societal marketing concept*, which flows from pure marketing, the enterprise should determine the needs, wants, and interests of target markets. It should then deliver superior value to customers in a way that maintains or improves the consumer's and society's well-being. Societal marketing orientation is the newest of the marketing management orientations.

A societal marketing orientation questions whether the pure marketing concept as it stands is adequate in an age of environmental problems, resource shortages, rapid population growth, worldwide economic problems and neglected social services.

It asks if the company that senses, serves, and satisfies individual wants is always doing what is best for consumers and society in the long run. According to the societal marketing concept, the pure marketing concept overlooks possible conflicts between consumer short-term wants and consumer long-term welfare[16].

## COCA COLA'S MARKETING ACTIVITIES – TWO SIDES OF THE SAME COIN

Consider the Coca-Cola Company. Most people see it as a highly responsible corporation producing fine soft drinks that satisfy consumer tastes. Yet some consumer and environmental groups have voiced concerns that Coke has little nutritional value, can harm people's teeth, contains caffeine, and adds to the litter problem with disposable bottles and cans.

Source: Kotler, P. and Armstrong, G. 1996. *Principles of Marketing.* 7th edition. Englewood, Cliffs, NJ: Prentice Hall, p 19.

Such concerns and conflicts led to the societal marketing concept. As Figure 1.2 indicates, the societal marketing concept requires marketers to balance three considerations in setting their marketing policies: company profits, consumer wants and society's interests.

## FIGURE 1.2 THREE CONSIDERATIONS UNDERLYING THE SOCIETAL MARKETING CONCEPT

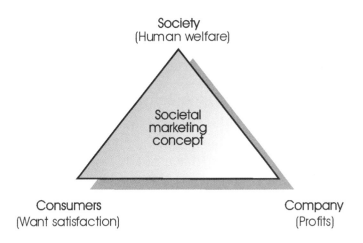

Source: Kotler, P and Armstrong, G. 1996. *Principles of marketing.* 7th ed. Englewood Cliffs, NJ: Prentice Hall, p 19.

Originally, most businesses based their marketing decisions largely on short-term company profit.

Eventually, they began to recognise the longer-term importance of satisfying consumer wants, and the marketing concept emerged. Now many enterprises are beginning to think of society's interests first when making their marketing decisions. Johnson and Johnson is one such company. The company backs its words with actions.

> Consider the Tylenol tampering case, in which eight people died from swallowing cyanide-laced capsules of Tylenol, a Johnson & Johnson brand. Although J & J believed that the pills had been altered in only a few stores, not in the factory, it quickly recalled all of its product. The recall cost the company $240 million in earnings. In the long run, however, the company's swift recall of Tylenol strengthened consumer confidence and loyalty, and Tylenol remains one of the nation's leading brands of pain reliever.

In this and other cases, J & J management has found that doing what is right benefits both consumers and the company. Thus, over the years, Johnson & Johnson's dedication to consumers and community service has made it one of America's most admired companies, and one of the most profitable[17].

Nowadays, marketers are looking a little further and aim to forge long-term relationships with certain groups (customers, shareholders, and so on). This forging of long-term relationships with certain groups can be defined as *relationship marketing*.

## 1.5   RELATIONSHIP MARKETING[18]

### 1.5.1   A broader view of the market

Relationship marketing logically follows from the gradual development of marketing thought. Relationship marketing is not a new theme, as many of the elements involved have already been mentioned in this chapter. Relationship marketing places its main focus on the maintenance of long-term relationships between the business, the government, the public, suppliers of raw materials, employees, and current and potential consumers. Everybody employed in all sections of the business must co-operate to ensure the fullest possible consumer satisfaction with product quality and service excellence. This is crucial for survival and growth, especially in an economic decline and in order to protect the competitive position. Relationship marketing means that the market offering must be expanded in order to successfully differentiate it from those of competitors and to ensure a greater degree of consumer satisfaction.

Relationship marketing evolved because so many businesses were paying only lip service to the marketing concept and where the attitudes of management did not clearly reflect the principles of the marketing concept.

Relationship marketing represents a broader view of the market and the marketing task. The details are discussed in subsequent paragraphs.

## 1.5.2  Expansion of the market offering

According to Christopher, Payne and Ballantyne,[19] relationship marketing means that the four marketing instruments alone are inadequate to ensure full consumer satisfaction. The writers concluded that two further variables, namely *people* and *processes*, must be added to the four existing marketing instruments. The *people* are the employees, who should be well trained in customer service, and must realise that their own job satisfaction ultimately rests on the success of the business in the market. *Processes* are integral parts of the production, administration and marketing functions. For example, the quality of the physical product is directly related to the production processes, while it is the quality of the physical product plus customer service activities that provide full consumer satisfaction. This means, therefore, that there must be a very close relationship between the marketing and production functions. The writers mentioned above refer to the marketing department as the 'smile department', but it must be clear that friendliness and willingness can never compensate for a low-quality product or one that does not serve its purpose. It is only when synergy has been achieved between all the processes that consumer satisfaction can be ensured. Synergy means that the whole is worth more than the sum of its parts. When all the variables support each other they reinforce the quality image of the product. The TQM principle underlies relationship marketing. TQM refers to 'Total Quality Management', which guarantees consumer satisfaction. However, this can only be an ideal of perfection and is closely related to the corporate culture where everybody must make an effort to realise this ideal.

> ## TQM as applied by Panasonic
>
> Panasonic's slogan points to this ideal of 'perfection':
>
> 'The quest for zero defect'

### 1.5.3 A bigger market

Relationship marketing also entails a wider view of the market itself. In the total market there are various smaller groupings, all with a greater or lesser influence on the marketing effort.

Close relationships, especially with important groupings, must be maintained. The following groups can be identified:

- Current customers, whose loyalty is crucially important.

- Potential customers in unexploited markets, who must be contacted.

- Suppliers, who must be made aware of the importance of their co-operation in order to fully satisfy the needs of consumers. Suppliers contribute by timely delivery of quality raw materials, components, and services. The excuse for bad customer service is so often that the spare parts/stock needed have not yet arrived, ignoring customer convenience.

- Potential employees, who must be carefully selected according to their abilities and especially their attitude towards customer service. Good employees prefer to work for successful companies.

- Reference groups who can convey the marketing message by direct personal contact ('word-of-mouth advertising'). The advantages of brand-loyal consumers, who not only repeatedly purchase the product but who also advise friends to do so, can never be underestimated.

- The influencers such as government, who may be able to exert an influence on the marketing activities of the business.

- Current employees, who are part of the internal market. Management has a responsibility to train, motivate and remunerate employees but must, furthermore, also persuade these employees to actively support marketing decisions and strategies. For this purpose there must be open and free communication and employees should hear about products and plans right from the beginning. It very often happens that an employee is unaware of the business's new advertising campaign until confronted with it on the television screen. Sometimes new products are noticed for the first time on the supermarket shelf. When something like this happens, the business loses out on input in terms of employee enthusiasm and willingness.

  A subtle persuasive approach to the internal marketing programme is preferable to a more aggressive one, as a persuasive approach contributes to the creation of a beneficial corporate culture (the prevailing climate in which employees must perform their duties). If the attitude of employees is negative, it will be reflected in their actions. Employees come into contact with consumers as well as reference groups, other potential employees, suppliers and even the influencers. They must be trained in internal marketing programmes to approach these markets in the correct way.

## EXAMPLES OF POOR CUSTOMER SERVICE

- Sales personnel chatting to each other while customers are waiting.

- Sales personnel being disinterested or condescending or those who make the customer feel unwelcome in any way.

- Employees who are careless or incompetent.

- Promises made/delivery dates not kept.

- Inadequate or incorrect information in advertising messages.

- Receptionists who are unwilling or unable to handle telephone enquiries.

- Personnel in banks drinking tea and eating in full view of long queues of people.

- Appointments not kept on time.

- Employees being overly friendly to customers.

There are many other examples of poor customer service which can be regarded as dishonest, such as padding repair costs. Anything that smacks of dishonesty is not marketing and is therefore not the topic under discussion in this book.

Handling customer complaints is an important facet of an internal marketing programme. Some car manufacturers have a customer care number with a direct line to the managing director. It is important for companies to research the reasons for complaints. The best and cheapest solution is to ensure that there are no complaints. Well-founded complaints must receive immediate attention. There must be ample opportunities for customers to direct complaints to responsible people who are able to take appropriate corrective action and, in so doing, prevent the loss of customers.

Consumers who are reluctant to complain but rather tend to avoid the unsatisfactory product or the situation in future are a grave threat to successful marketing. Consumers who are unhappy and who receive no satisfaction can also direct their complaints to the many consumer-action programmes (for example, the Isobel Jones column in the Sunday Times) in the mass media, thereby causing unwelcome negative publicity for the enterprise.

Relationship marketing is, in fact, the essence of a market-driven approach to marketing management.

It has been said previously that the evolution process will probably continue necessitating further adaptations in marketing thought.

## 1.6 DEFINING MARKETING[20]

So far, marketing has not been clearly defined. This is by design, as it is imperative to first have a good understanding of the nature and extent of the marketing process. Whilst it is true that no two writers agree on the exact formulation of a good definition for this complicated process, the following definition will serve as a good foundation.

> Marketing is a combination of management tasks and decisions aimed at meeting opportunities and threats in a dynamic environment in such a way that its market offerings lead to the satisfaction of consumers' needs and wants in such a way that the objectives of the business, the consumer and society are achieved.

The key words in this definition are described in Figure 1.3.

### FIGURE 1.3 KEY WORDS IN THE DEFINITION OF MARKETING

| | |
|---|---|
| MANAGEMENT TASKS | Planning, implementation and control. |
| DECISIONS | Regarding product, distribution, marketing communication methods and price (4 Ps). |
| OPPORTUNITIES | Favourable circumstances in the marketing environment which must be utilised by marketing management. |
| THREATS | Unfavourable conditions which marketing management must endeavour to change into opportunities. |

| DYNAMIC ENVIRONMENT | Continually changing environmental variables which necessitate appropriate reaction from marketing management. |
|---|---|
| NEED-SATISFYING | Properties of a product based on what the consumer wants. |
| MARKET OFFERING | Product, price, distribution, marketing communication as well as service by people and processes. |
| ATTAINMENT OF OBJECTIVES | |
| ■ the enterprise | Maximisation of profitability in the long term. |
| ■ the consumer | Need satisfaction within the resources and abilities of the business. |
| ■ society | Ensuring the well-being of society in the longer term. |

It is now time to look at the broader picture of what marketing entails. It can be seen as a process.

## 1.7  THE MARKETING PROCESS [21]

The marketing process, which has evolved from a simple bartering transaction between two participants, has become a very complex task. In a large business there  is usually a marketing department which is responsible for the marketing task. Heading this department is a Marketing Manager and team of specialists involved in the marketing task. All the activities discussed in the previous section must be performed by the marketing department in such a way as to ensure the maximum advantage for the company as a whole. This is not easy to do! Follow the description of the marketing process in Figure 1.4.

There are four variables about which the marketing management team must take decisions: the *product* itself, the *place* where it is to be sold (distribution of the product), the *marketing communication* methods to be used to inform the consumer, and the *price* of the product, which should reflect its value to the consumer. The four variables combine in a market offering which the consumer may decide to buy if it provides satisfaction of his or her needs. These four variables are known as the marketing instruments. They are also known as the marketing mix, consisting of four 'Ps' (product, place, promotion or marketing communication, and price). Decisions regarding the four marketing instruments combine to form an integrated marketing strategy (or marketing plan).

The marketing strategy for a specific market offering is directed at a group of consumers in a specific environment. If anything should change in the environment, the market offering and the marketing strategy must be changed accordingly.

It is a fact that the market offering is seldom directed at the satisfaction of one single consumer; rather a group of people is usually involved. The larger this group, usually the more advantageous it is for the manufacturer and the intermediaries. In the total consumer market there are many different groups. The members of each of these groups (also called **market segments**) have more or less similar characteristics, needs and product preferences. After careful consideration, marketing management selects, from many different market segments, a specific target market (or markets). The market offering is often changed in some way or another to meet the preferences of different target markets. It seldom happens that an enterprise has only one single target market.

Recent trends in marketing have introduced new concepts such as **mass customisation**, implying that the Internet can be used to develop a marketing strategy for a single consumer.

## THE MARKETING PROCESS IN NON–PROFIT–SEEKING BUSINESS

In non-profit-seeking businesses (for example, the Cancer Association), the main objective is not profit but rather effectiveness. The association strives to achieve, at the lowest possible cost, results in terms of patient care, advice and research as well as in fundraising activities. All four marketing instruments are used for this purpose. The 'product' here is an idea (prevent cancer) explained in brochures and stickers. The 'product' is distributed by the branch offices of the Cancer Association in different towns. Marketing communication is provided by fundraisers in personal contact and by means of advertising in the mass media. The contribution made to the fund is the sacrifice made by donors and the price that must be paid.

There are usually also a number of competitors marketing similar products and competing for the patronage of the same target markets. Market offerings often differ only slightly from one another, perhaps only in different brand names. Consumers select – and purchase repeatedly – those brand names that afford them the greatest need satisfaction in terms of the sacrifice that they must make. Often the sacrifice is not only in monetary terms; sometimes consumers are also willing to suffer some degree of inconvenience to obtain the desired brand name product.

## FIGURE 1.4 THE MARKETING PROCESS

Source: Van der Walt, A; Strydom, JW; Marx, S and Jooste, CJ. 1996. *Marketing management.* 3rd edition. Cape Town: Juta, p 11.

The preceding rather complex explanation is illustrated in Figure 1.4, which shows the marketing process in a profit-seeking business. Note the way the arrows link the environment, marketing management and the target market. Environmental changes influence both marketing management and the target market while marketing management is dependent on the feedback received from the market and the environment.

It is important to place in the correct perspective the marketing function as performed in a modern enterprise.

## 1.8 THE MARKETING FUNCTION IN THE BUSINESS [22]

### 1.8.1 The place of the marketing function

The marketing function can be regarded as a key function in the business because of its contribution to profit and its closeness to the consumers. Seven different functional departments can be identified in the modern large business. The managers heading these seven departments must work together to realise the business's objectives. A typical functional organisational structure is shown in Figure 1.5.

### FIGURE 1.5 FUNCTIONAL ORGANISATIONAL STRUCTURE

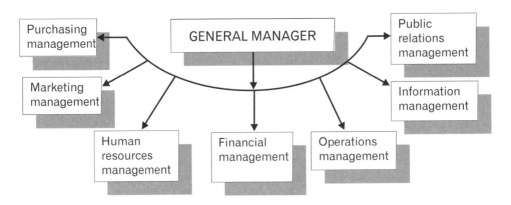

The functions of the departments in Figure 1.5 are described as follows:

■ The *operations function* comprises the physical utilisation of raw materials and components and their conversion into manufactured materials and finished products, usually found in a factory.

- The ***human resources function*** pertains to the acquisition, training, utilisation and retaining of a sufficient number of competent personnel.

- The ***financial function*** includes the acquisition, utilisation and control of the funds necessary for running the business. The main activities here are the acquisition and application of funds for the profitability, liquidity, solvency and continuity of the business.

- The ***purchasing function*** ensures that the materials necessary for production are bought at the right places, at the right times, in the right quantities and at the right prices.

- The ***public relations function*** maintains and cultivates a favourable and objective image of the business among those whose opinion is important to the achievement of the business's objectives.

- The ***information function*** makes available internal information for planning and control.

- The ***marketing function*** generates income from sales and is responsible for managing the marketing process.

- ***General management*** includes the activities of people in managerial positions. The people in top, middle and lower management have to plan for, organise, lead and control the business as a whole as well as its individual functions. The general manager is at the head of the management team.

In practice, there are also other functions and structures, and indeed other names may be used. It is important, however, to realise that the tasks of the different functional departments must be performed in both large and small businesses. The resources (capital) and abilities of various functionaries determine the existence and size of formal departments.

In very large multi-product businesses there can be even more different divisions than those shown in Figure 1.5. There can be, for example, a marketing director directing several marketing managers for different products or product ranges. The marketing director provides leadership and co-ordinates the activities of several different marketing departments.

What does a manager do? The workers tend to think that managers spend their working hours by sitting and talking while there is real work to be done. However, there are four management tasks which must be performed by the management team.

## 1.8.2 The management tasks in marketing

The management tasks consist of a continuous process of planning, organising, leading and controlling marketing activities. Marketing management is responsible for the following:

- Identifying opportunities and threats in the marketing environment.

- Identifying those opportunities which can be utilised in terms of internal strengths and weaknesses.

- Compiling marketing data.

- Selecting a specific target market.

- Deciding on the products to be produced in order to satisfy consumer needs.

- Deciding on the selling price of the product in order to attain the objective of profitability.

- Deciding on specific distribution channels.

- Deciding on marketing communication methods whereby consumers are informed, reminded and persuaded.

- Deciding on selection, training, remuneration and motivation of marketing personnel.

- Organising and leading the activities of the marketing department.

- Controlling the marketing process.

These responsibilities are part of the four management tasks which are summarised in Figure 1.6 and discussed below.

- *Planning*

    Planning by marketing management entails the examination of and the choice between various ways of utilising marketing opportunities, countering marketing threats and achieving marketing objectives. Marketing decisions thus begin with the identification and evaluation of marketing opportunities and threats, and internal strengths and weaknesses.

## FIGURE 1.6  THE MANAGEMENT TASKS OF MARKETING MANAGEMENT

| PLANNING | | |
|---|---|---|
| Identify opportunities and threats | Set marketing objectives according to business's objectives | Decide on the marketing instruments |
| Consider the internal strong and weak points | | |

**IMPLEMENTATION**

- Organising

  Organise and co-ordinate the activities in the marketing department.

- Leading

  Provide leadership in planning and implementation of marketing strategies

**CONTROL/EVALUATION**

Set standards and measure performance.

Source: Adapted from Van der Walt, A; Strydom, JW, Marx, S and Jooste,CJ. 1996. *Marketing management*. 3rd edition. Cape Town: Juta, p 14.

### ■ Implementation

***Organising and co-ordinating*** calls for the creation of an organisational structure best suited to the implementation of the marketing decisions in order to achieve marketing objectives. Marketing activities are grouped rationally and individual divisions and managers are tasked with carrying them out. Finally, the levels of authority, areas of responsibility, lines of communication and methods of co-ordination between the divisions and individuals are determined. Co-operation is achieved by integrating the interests of divisions, individuals, consumers, investors, suppliers and the community as a whole.

Figure 1.7 shows a typical organisation chart of the different divisions in the marketing department under the leadership of the marketing manager.

### FIGURE 1.7  FUNCTIONAL MARKETING ORGANISATION

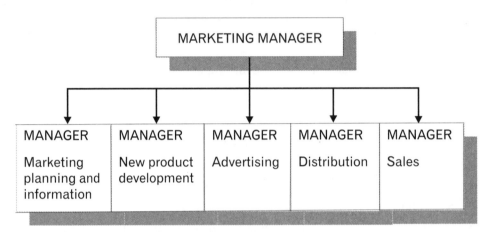

*Leading* involves a wide range of tasks, such as staffing, communicating and motivating. From a marketing viewpoint, leading embraces all the marketing decisions for putting preparation (planning, organising, co-ordinating and controlling) into practice. Briefly, once the marketing strategy has been formulated, people have to be found to perform the required marketing activities (staffing); they have to be instructed as to what they should do and told how well they are doing it (communicating) and a positive attitude towards work and the enterprise must be carefully cultivated and maintained (motivating). Leading is therefore of paramount importance in the effective performance of the other management tasks.

### ■ *Control*

*Controlling or evaluation* is the regulatory task of marketing management, and its purpose is to align actual performance with marketing plans. In order to exercise control, it is essential first to set standards, which requires determination of what has to be controlled and where marketing control is necessary. Secondly, actual marketing performance has to be measured and compared with these standards. Thirdly, the differences between actual performance and standards have to be evaluated. Finally, if necessary, corrective measures should be taken to ensure that future performance is in line with marketing plans.

If marketing management does not perform the management tasks properly:

- purchasing management will not know which raw materials and components to purchase;

- public relations management will not know how to perform or improve its liaison function;

- financial management will now know how much funding is required; and

- human resources management will not know how many people to employ.

## 1.9  MARKETING CHALLENGES THAT LIE AHEAD[23]

The marketing environment is dynamic and global. The new century will once again produce challenges for marketers. Rapid changes can quickly make yesterday's winning strategies obsolete.

What are the marketing challenges as we head into the twenty-first century? Today's companies are wrestling with changing customer values and orientations; economic stagnation; environmental decline; increased global competition; and a host of other economic, political, and social problems. However, these problems also provide marketing opportunities. We now look more deeply into several key trends and forces that are changing the marketing landscape and challenging marketing strategy: growth of non-profit marketing, rapid globalisation, the changing world economy, and the call for more socially responsible actions[24].

### 1.9.1  Growth of non-profit marketing

In recent years, marketing has become a major component in the strategies of many non-profit organisations, such as colleges, hospitals, museums, symphony orchestras and even churches. The arts, and museums in South Africa in particular, have been hit by severe cutbacks in government allocations. In the same way, many hospitals in South Africa have closed down because of a lack of funds. These institutions now have to find their own funds and they need to become more marketing-oriented. The continued growth of non-profit and public sector marketing presents new and exciting challenges for marketing managers.

## 1.9.2 Globalisation[25]

Geographical and cultural distances have shrunk with the advent of jet aeroplanes, telefax machines, global computer and telephone hook-ups, world television satellite broadcasts, and especially the phenomenal worldwide growth in access to and use of the Internet. This has allowed companies to expand their geographical market coverage enormously. The result is a vastly more complex marketing environment, for both companies and consumers.

Today, almost every company, large or small, is affected in some way by global competition. Think about the many small importers in South Africa selling computers, toys and other items. South African companies have been challenged at home by the entry to the South African market of many competitors from the United States of America and Asia since 1994.

Companies around the world are asking: Just what is global marketing? How does it differ from domestic marketing? How do global competitors and forces affect our business? To what extent should we 'go global'? Many companies are forming strategic alliances with foreign companies, even competitors, who serve as suppliers or marketing partners. The past few years have produced some surprising alliances between competitors such as BMW and Rover, Mercedes-Benz and Chrysler. Winning companies in the next century may well be those that have built the best global networks.

## 1.9.3 The changing world economy[26]

The past few decades have seen the world in general growing poorer. A sluggish world economy has resulted in more difficult times for both consumers and marketers.

Around the world, people's needs are greater than ever, but in many areas people lack the means to pay for needed goods. In South Africa, this has been harsh. Although wages have risen, real buying power has declined, especially for the less-skilled members of the workforce. Many workers have lost their jobs as manufacturers have 'downsized' to cut costs. In all sectors of the economy, jobs have been lost. Current economic conditions create both problems and opportunities for marketers. Some companies are facing declining demand and see few opportunities for growth. Others, however, are developing new solutions for dealing with consumer problems. Many are finding ways to offer consumers 'more for less'.

### 1.9.4  The call for a more ethical approach and social responsibility[27]

A third factor in today's marketing environment is the increased call for companies to take responsibility for the social and environmental impact of their actions. Corporate ethics has become a hot topic in almost every business arena.

The ethics and environmental movements will place even stricter demands on companies in the future, and companies will be held to an increasingly higher standard of environmental responsibility in their marketing and manufacturing activities.

### 1.9.5  The new marketing landscape: value to customers

The past decade has taught businesses everywhere a humbling lesson. Domestic companies learned that they can no longer ignore global markets and competitors. Successful businesses in mature industries found that they cannot overlook emerging markets, technologies and management approaches. Companies of every sort learned that they cannot remain inwardly focused, ignoring the needs of customers and their environment[28].

'As we move into the next century, companies will have to become customer-oriented and market driven in all that they do. It is not enough to be product or technology driven – too many companies will design their products without customer input, only to find them rejected in the marketplace. It is not enough to be good at winning new customers – too many companies forget about customers after the sale, only to lose their future business. The key to success in the rapidly changing marketing environment will be a strong focus on the marketplace and a total marketing commitment to providing value to customers'[29].

---

SUMMARY

A business does not operate in isolation, and many factors contribute to the success of a company. Marketing is a managerial process aimed at satisfying the needs and wants of customers. These needs and wants are met by creating the correct products and services. Marketing operates within a dynamic global environment, and is facing new challenges as we approach the turn of the century.

---

The success of the marketing concept is now widely understood, spurring growth in non-profit marketing as these organisations begin using the tools and techniques of marketing management. The environment is changing as well, with almost every company being affected by rapid globalisation. The changing world economy, which has been sluggish for a long time, has resulted in more difficult times for both consumers and marketers. These challenges are intensified by a demand that marketers conduct all of their business with an emphasis on more ethical processes and social responsibility. Taken together, these changes define a new marketing landscape. Companies that succeed in this environment will have a strong focus on the changing marketplace and a total commitment to using the tools of marketing to provide real value to customers[30].

## REFERENCES

1.  Based on Lamb, CW; Hair, JF and McDaniel, C. 1998. *Marketing*. 4th edition. Ohio: SouthWestern College Publishing, p 4.
2.  Lamb *et al* p 4.
3.  Lamb *et al* p 4.
4.  Lamb *et al* p 4.
5.  Lamb *et al* p 4.
6.  Busch, PS and Houston, MJ. 1985. *Marketing: Strategic foundations*. Homewood, Ill: Richard D Irwin Inc., p 15.
7.  Van der Walt, A; Strydom, JW; Marx, S and Jooste, CJ. 1996. *Marketing management*. 3rd edition. Cape Town: Juta, pp 6 – 7.
8.  Largely taken from Lamb *et al*, pp 5 – 7.
9.  Lamb *et al*, p 6.    Based on Kotler *et al* p 16.
10. Based on Lamb *et al*, p 5.
11. Lamb *et al*, p 6.
12. Lamb *et al*, p 6.
13. Van der Walt *et al* p 20.
14. Based on  Van der Walt *et al* pp 20 – 27.
15. Kotler, P and Armstrong, G.1996. *Principles of marketing*. 7th edition. Englewood Cliffs, NJ: Prentice Hall, pp 19 – 20.
16. Kotler and Armstrong, p 19.
17. Kotler and Armstrong, p 20.
18. Based on Van der Walt *et al* pp 27 – 30.
19. Christopher, M; Payne, A and Ballantyne, D. 1991. *Relationship Marketing*. Oxford: Heineman, p 8.
20. Taken from Van der Walt *et al* p 32.
21. Taken from Van der Walt *et al* pp 8 – 11.
22. Taken from Van der Walt *et al* pp 12 – 16.
23. Taken from Kotler and Armstrong, pp 20 – 26.
24. Taken from Kotler and Armstrong, p 22.
25. Taken from Kotler and Armstrong, p 22.

26. Taken from Kotler and Armstrong, p 24.

27. Taken from Kotler and Armstrong, p 24.

28. Taken from Kotler and Armstrong, p 25.

29. Taken from Kotler and Armstrong, p 25.

30. Taken from Kotler and Armstrong, p 26.

# CHAPTER 2

## THE MARKETING ENVIRONMENT

## 2.1  INTRODUCTION

The previous chapter mentioned, *inter alia*, that marketing involves the extensive task of profit-seeking businesses seeking profits to survive and grow at all costs in a highly competitive market. Because the contemporary business has existed in an extremely unstable and turbulent environment in the past decade or two, a marketer can only survive, grow and make a profit if management knows what is going on in the environment. Instead of changing slowly and at a predictable pace, as in earlier decades such as the 1950s, the environment in which marketers find themselves at present holds many surprises and shocks.

Who would have thought that the average rand exchange rate against the US dollar would decline from R2,85 in 1993 to R4,29 in 1996 and is currently hovering at R6,10. How many marketers realised ten years ago, in planning their communication, that the black newspaper, The Sowetan, would have the highest circulation in the country? How many marketers would have thought that the turmoil in markets in the East would have such a dramatic influence on the South African economy in 1998 and 1999?

Yet many marketers still do not realise the implications of this, especially when it comes to affirmative action, cultural and value shifts (which are becoming more Afrocentric), and the questions surrounding the future economic order. The surprises and shocks that the environment has in store for marketers are not confined to South Africa. Thus, for example, the American motor and electronics industries did not foresee Japan and other Asian countries' world domination of these industries.

The so-called 'surprises' that the environment produces are nothing more than trends that appear and disappear, only to reappear in a different guise at a later stage. These trends or external environmental variables largely determine the success of the business's marketing efforts.

Thus the position of consumers and competitors in the market, relations with suppliers, economic, social and political trends, and numerous other events prevailing in the environment will, from time to time, threaten the successful existence of the business or, conversely, offer receptive and favourable conditions with good marketing opportunities.

Marketing management, however, does not deal exclusively with the external variables. Although marketing is also one of the main functions of the business organisation and, in terms of the marketing concept, plays the principal role in its strategy formulation, the marketing activities should be performed in conjunction with other functional departments and according to specific directives from top management. These directives refer more specifically to the mission, objectives and overall strategies formulated by top management to be pursued and supported by all the functional departments, including marketing management. Marketing management must also work closely with other departments to implement the marketing strategy. Those variables that concern marketing management within the business are known as the *internal environmental variables*.

*The sum total of the variables and forces inside as well as outside the business which influence marketing management's decisions constitute the marketing environment*. This environment influences marketing management's ability to develop and execute successful strategies for its target market.

The successful management of marketing activities calls for an awareness on the part of marketing management of the internal and external variables which can affect the marketing efforts, and the marketing strategy, as indicated in Figure 2.1, should be adapted on an ongoing basis to tie in with changes in the environment. Internal scanning is therefore necessary to determine the enterprise's strengths and weaknesses. External scanning is also necessary to gauge opportunities and threats (the SWOT approach). Of course, the aim here is to deploy the business's strengths and resources in the market in such a way that it can fully utilise opportunities and ward off any threats timeously.

In essence, environmental scanning is part of the formulation of a marketing strategy and actually involves directing the business's resources towards satisfying the needs of the market.

## FIGURE 2.1 ENVIRONMENTAL VARIABLES AND MARKETING INSTRUMENTS

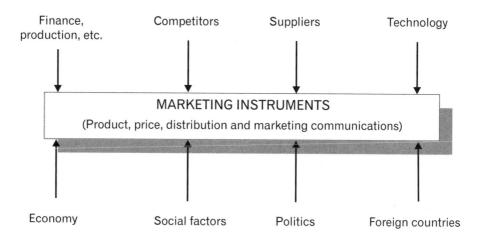

Timeous and continuous scanning (both inside and outside the business) of the total environment in which marketing management must operate is therefore a prerequisite for sound decision making about marketing strategy. Against the background of these introductory comments regarding the environment in which marketing management operates, the following outcomes are set:

LEARNING OUTCOMES

At the end of this chapter you will be able to:

■ explain the concept 'marketing environment';

■ explain the interfaces between marketing management and the environment, namely the role of marketing management, and opportunities and threats in the environment;

■ describe the composition of the marketing environment, namely the micro-, marketing and macro-environments, variables in the environment and their implication for marketing management; and

■ discuss a few methods of environmental scanning.

## 2.2 MARKETING MANAGEMENT AND THE MARKETING ENVIRONMENT [1]

### 2.2.1 Management and environmental change

The underlying problem for the successful survival of contemporary business in the Western world is the fact that the environment usually changes more quickly than the business is able to adapt. Hence the study of the marketing environment mainly revolves around change in the environment.

Change is a difficult term to define. Expressed simply, it is any alteration in the *status quo*. This implies a change from a condition of stability to one of instability – a shift from the predictable to the unpredictable. It cannot be measured and causes uncertainty. No single factor can be held responsible for change and, in different places and communities, it occurs in different ways and at different rates.

Technological innovation, economic fluctuations, changing social values and demographic trends, political change, aggressive international competition and countless other variables are constantly changing the marketing environment, to such an extent that they affect not only the performance of business detrimentally but also threaten their existence. During the past decade, the structure of South African society and its lifestyles, values and expectations have changed perceptibly. Increasingly Afrocentric characteristics which will dominate the South African environment in the first decades of 2000 are beginning to appear. As a component of the environment, business expansion is therefore at the centre of environmental change and is constantly exposed to change. The end result of this change is a new environment with new trends which can be classified into three groups, namely:

■ Trends which constitute opportunites for marketing management – that is, *a favourable situation in the environment in which the business has a competitive advantage and has the necessary resources to utilise it*. The main advantages resulting from change are probably the creation of new markets and the broadening of existing ones.

■ Trends which pose particular threats to marketing management – that is, *an unfavourable situation in the environment which, if it is allowed to go unchecked, may have a detrimental effect on the performance or survival of the business*.

■ Trends which may appear but which have **no implications** for the business or the industry.

---

### The Swiss watch industry and the threat of new (and unexpected) competition

The following table shows how the market share of the Swiss watch industry which, in 1948, was responsible for 80% of all watches sold in the world, has shrunk to a mere 13%.

#### ANALYSIS OF THE WORLD PRODUCTION OF WATCHES

| Year | World production (in millions) | Switzerland % | Japan % | Hong Kong % | USA % | Rest of World % |
|---|---|---|---|---|---|---|
| 1948 | 31 | 80 | – | – | – | 20 |
| 1970 | 174 | 43 | 14 | – | 11 | 32 |
| 1975 | 218 | 34 | 14 | 2 | 12 | 38 |
| 1980 | 300 | 29 | 22 | 20 | 4 | 25 |
| 1985 | 440 | 13 | 39 | 22 | 0,4 | 25 |

The threat, which came as a surprise for the Swiss watch industry, can be ascribed to the following facts (inadequate environmental scanning):

1. The inability of the Swiss to acknowledge that there was considerable growth in the cheaper segments of the market.

2. An inability to read the implications of new technology properly. The primary concern here is the speed at which mechanically-driven watches have been replaced by quartz watches. In 1974, 98% of all watches were still mechanical, while in 1984, 76% were quartz and only 24% mechanical.

3. Poor scanning of international competition, especially Asian competition.

The question that arises here is to what extent Swiss watchmakers would have been able to counter the attack if they had scanned the environment and identified major technological and competitive threats.

---

Source: Wilson, RM and Gilligan, C. 1997. *Strategic marketing management.* 2nd edition. London: Butterworths Heinemann, p 243.

Successful businesses that adapt to the environment are those that constantly scan the environment and adjust their strategies to keep abreast of change.

Adjusting strategies is therefore nothing more than those steps which marketing management takes to gain a particular environmental fit for the business. Successful marketers do not delay their strategy adjustments until the environment has changed so drastically that nothing can be done about it. They continually scan the environment and management proactively.

A few comments on the role of marketing management in environmental scanning are necessary before the composition of the environment is examined.

## 2.2.2   Marketing management and the environment

Although the interaction between the business and its environment is the concern of the entire strategic management team, marketing management probably plays the most important role in this interaction. Support for this argument can be found, *firstly*, in the existence of a business mission statement, an important component which examines the business's product-market relationship. This entails a broad but clear indication of the business, product or service and at what market it is aimed. Both the business's product development and its market fall within the domain of marketing management, which necessitates its involvement in the development of the business's mission and strategy, as well as its involvement with the external environment.

A *second* reason for the importance of marketing management's involvement in the interaction between the business and its environment arises from the requirements that the marketing concept puts to management. It calls upon top management to determine the needs of the consumer and to satisfy them instead of deciding for the consumer what he/she needs.

*Thirdly*, marketing management plays a decisive role in the interface between the business and its environment because the latest trends in strategic management show that successful businesses are externally oriented – that is, they focus on the consumer, the competitor, the market and the market's environment.

One should also bear in mind that corporate planners depend on marketing management for ideas on new products and marketing opportunities and that the marketing strategy (product, price, distribution and marketing communication) plays a decisive role in the total strategy.

The question that arises is how marketing management should become aware of and scan the infinite number of variables that can influence decision making. This is possible only if marketing management classifies and scans the numerous variables meaningfully. Before concentrating on scanning methods, it is necessary to conduct a meaningful classification of the variables in the marketing environment.

The composition of the environment in which marketing management operates, also called the marketing environment, will be discussed next.

## 2.3  THE COMPOSITION OF THE MARKETING ENVIRONMENT

The introductory definition of the marketing environment stated that it is the sum total of the factors or variables and players which influence the ability of marketing management to successfully develop strategies for its target market. In order to scrutinise the multiplicity of environmental variables that influence marketing management, it is necessary to conduct a meaningful *classification* of the marketing environment to identify certain trends for further analysis in each group of *sub-environment*. Figure 2.2 shows the composition of the marketing environment. It is clear from this figure that the total marketing environment comprises three principal components: the micro-, marketing and macro-environments. Each of these will now be examined.

## 2.4  THE MICRO-ENVIRONMENT

The first component of the total environment is the micro-environment or the internal environment, which comprises the business organisation itself. Although this refers to those variables which are largely controlled by the business itself, such as its mission and objectives, its management structure, its resources and culture, one should remember that these variables are not solely under the control of marketing management.

As already mentioned, marketing management does have a significant influence on these variables and marketing provides the central input in developing overall strategies, but it should be clear that while top management controls certain micro-variables, marketing management can also control some variables in the micro-environment.

## FIGURE 2.2 COMPOSITION OF THE MARKETING ENVIRONMENT

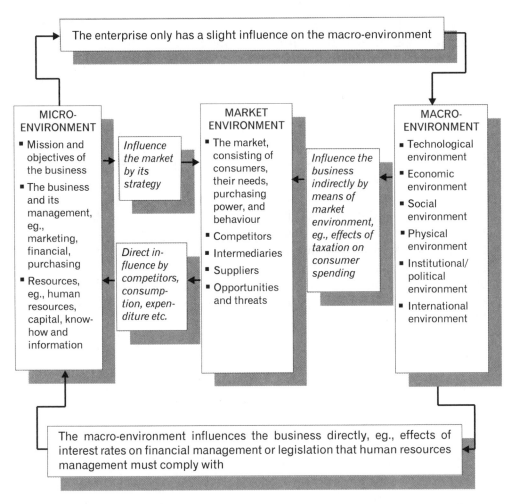

The enterprise only has a slight influence on the macro-environment

| MICRO-ENVIRONMENT | | MARKET ENVIRONMENT | | MACRO-ENVIRONMENT |
|---|---|---|---|---|
| ▪ Mission and objectives of the business | *Influence the market by its strategy* | ▪ The market, consisting of consumers, their needs, purchasing power, and behaviour | *Influence the business indirectly by means of market environment, eg., effects of taxation on consumer spending* | ▪ Technological environment |
| ▪ The business and its management, eg., marketing, financial, purchasing | | | | ▪ Economic environment |
| | | | | ▪ Social environment |
| | | ▪ Competitors | | ▪ Physical environment |
| | *Direct influence by competitors, consumption, expenditure etc.* | ▪ Intermediaries | | ▪ Institutional/political environment |
| ▪ Resources, eg., human resources, capital, know-how and information | | ▪ Suppliers | | ▪ International environment |
| | | ▪ Opportunities and threats | | |

The macro-environment influences the business directly, eg., effects of interest rates on financial management or legislation that human resources management must comply with

Source: Cronje, GJ de J *et al* (eds). 1994. *Introduction to business management.* Johannesburg: Southern, p 46.

Although **top management**, that is the executive management, which includes the functional managers, mainly focus their decision making on the organisation's mission, objectives and overall strategies, there are four basic top management decisions which are of particular importance for marketing management: the **basic line of business** (product or service) of the business, the **overall goals** of the business, **the role of marketing management** in the above and **the role of the other management** functions in reaching the overall goals. Table 2.1 gives a brief description of the four basic decisions taken by top management.

## TABLE 2.1  Variables in the micro-environment controlled by top management[2]

| VARIABLE | ALTERNATIVES |
|---|---|
| 1. Basic line of business (product or service) | |
| ■ Product/service category | Tourism, fast food, clothing, hotel industry,computers |
| ■ Technology category | Manufacturing, distributor, wholesaler |
| ■ Geographic category | Neighbourhood, city, region, province, national, international |
| ■ Ownership category | Sole proprietor, partnership, close corparation, public corparation |
| ■ Specific business category | City Lodge (hotel industry, national) Premier foods (food, manufacture, national) Hatfield Bakery (bakery industry, Pretoria only) |
| 2. Overal goals | |
| ■ Sales | Certain percentage increase per year or percentage market share |
| ■ Profit | Minimum percentage gross on net profit (on sales), profit ratios per product (patents), geographic area or rate of return on investment |
| ■ Customer acceptance | Environmentally-friendly products and socially responsible products (toys and medicine) |
| 3. The role of marketing management | |
| ■ Importance in the business | Line or staff functions, extensive budget and resources, role in strategy formulation |
| ■ Functions | Market research, planning, distribution, franchising |
| ■ Integration | Integration, decentralisation |
| 4. The role of the other management functions | |
| ■ Human resources management ■ Financial management ■ Operations management ■ Purchasing management | Determine responsibilities of each function, position of each in the organisational structure, relationship between functions, eg., should operations management be responsible for purchasing or should purchasing do the procurement? |

The decisions controlled by top management ultimately reflect the mission and overall goals of the business organisation.

From these top management decisions, marketing management must determine the variables for which it is responsible. Table 2.2 briefly illustrates the micro-variables which fall under its control. In order to manage these variables effectively, marketing management must be well informed about the business's mission and top management's decisions regarding the overall goals and strategies.

Marketing management must therefore constantly scan the micro-environment. Marketing management's activities should also complement and support top management's decisions if the business is to function as a unit.

### TABLE 2.2 Variables in the micro-environment controlled by marketing management[3]

| VARIABLE | ALTERNATIVES |
|---|---|
| 1. Selection of target market | |
| ■ Size | Mass market, specific market segment, geographic area |
| ■ Characteristics | Male, female, young, old, conservative, liberal, East or West |
| 2. Marketing objectives | |
| ■ Sales | Brand loyalty, new products, new markets |
| ■ Profit | Profit ratio per product, area, quantity |
| ■ Image | Quality, friendly, service |
| ■ Competitiveness | Competitive advantage through better product, lower price, extensive marketing comunication |
| 3. Organisational structure | |
| ■ Type | Functional, product, area |
| 4. Marketing plan | |
| ■ Product / service | One basic model, one colour, sizes, styles |
| ■ Distribution | Direct, wholesale, cybermarketing\E-commerce |
| ■ Price | High, low, skimming |
| ■ Marketing communication | Advertising, personal selling, publicity |
| 5. Control | Audit, cost analysis, control systems |

In the introductory chapter, it was stated that marketing management's task mainly revolves around supplying an attractive product or service for target markets to provide a particular return for the business. It is clear from the above brief discussion of the micro-environment that marketing management's success is influenced mainly by what happens in the rest of the business organisation, as well as occurrences in the market and macro-environments which affect the marketing effort. Hence marketing managers must not only study the needs of the target market but must also consider other variables and interest groups (functions) in the business organisation, namely top management, financial management, operations management, purchasing management, and so on. All of these related interest groups constitute a business's internal or micro-environment.

Management decisions – including those made by marketing management and other management areas – influence the market environment by extending or indeed curtailing the strategies employed to maintain the business's market share.

## 2.5 THE MARKET ENVIRONMENT

The second component of the marketing environment is the market environment, which is found just outside the business organisation. In this environment, all the variables depicted in Figure 2.2 are relevant to virtually every business because they determine the nature and strength of the competition in any industry. The key variables in this environment are the following:

- **Consumers** with a particular buying power and behaviour, which in turn determine the number of entrants to the market.

- **Competitors** who are established in the market and wish to maintain or improve their position, including existing, new and potential competitors.

- **Intermediaries** who compete against each other to handle the business's products, or wish to handle only those of competitors.

- **Suppliers** who provide or do not wish to provide products, raw materials, services and even financing to the business.

All these variables create particular **opportunities** and **threats**. Although marketing management can influence certain variables by adjusting its strategy, it has no control over these variables.

The market environment has a strong influence on the success or failure of the business. A case in point is a strong competitor who possesses the necessary ability to enter into a price war or launch a new substitute product. The principal task of marketing management in this environment is therefore to identify, evaluate and utilise opportunities that arise in the market and then to develop its strategies in order to meet competition. For these reasons, the market environment is also called the **task environment**. The market environment is also influenced by developments in the macro-environment, ultimately to reach the market environment.

### 2.5.1 Consumers

*The market consists of people with specific needs that have to be satisfied and who have the financial ability to satisfy them*.

This explains why consumers with their particular needs, buying power and behaviour are the chief component of the market environment. The market, or the consumers in the market environment, are in fact the ultimate target at which marketing management aims the business's market offering. In a study and analysis of the market (primarily by means of market research as discussed in chapter 3), marketing management should bear in mind that there are five groups of consumers or markets.

- **Consumer markets** in which individuals and households purchase products and services for personal consumption. In studying the consumer market, marketing management therefore firstly analyse the number of consumers in a particular area. The total South African consumer market, for example, is represented by the number of inhabitants. At the turn of the century, the population in South Africa is expected to increase to 46 million, with the following growth rates for each population group.

| Whites | 0,53% | Blacks | 2,26% |
| Coloureds | 1,26% | Asians | 1,20% |

Table 2.3 shows the distribution of the population across the nine provinces.

TABLE 2.3  Population of South Africa across the nine
            provinces, 1999

| PROVINCE | ASIANS | BLACKS | COLOUREDS | WHITES | TOTAL |
|---|---|---|---|---|---|
| EASTERN CAPE | 20 200 | 5 860 500 | 489 400 | 337 300 | 6 707 400 |
| FREE STATE | 2 900 | 2 388 700 | 82 400 | 322 700 | 2 796 700 |
| GAUTENG | 168 400 | 5 549 500 | 291 800 | 1 742 600 | 7 752 300 |
| KWAZULU–NATAL | 826 000 | 7 420 100 | 123 500 | 571 500 | 8 941 100 |
| MPUMALANGA | 13 600 | 2 686 900 | 21 200 | 258 800 | 2 980 500 |
| NORTHERN CAPE | 2 400 | 302 400 | 458 800 | 115 300 | 878 900 |
| NORTHERN PROVINCE | 5 700 | 5 130 700 | 8 200 | 120 500 | 5 265 100 |
| NORTH WEST | 10 500 | 3 287 600 | 48 700 | 227 300 | 3 574 100 |
| WESTERN CAPE | 43 200 | 912 300 | 2 299 900 | 860 900 | 4 116 300 |
| TOTAL RSA | 1 092 900 | 33 538 700 | 3 823 900 | 4 556 900 | 43 012 400 |

Source: Bureau for Marketing Research: Household expenditure in South Africa by province, population group and product, 1999, p 18.

Besides the number of consumers in a particular area or market segment analysed to estimate the market, a significant component of the consumer market is the **buying power** of the consumers. Buying power is represented mainly by the **personal disposable income** of consumers. Personal disposable income is that portion of personal income that remains after deducting direct tax, plus credit (loans from banks, shops and other institutions), which can therefore be used to purchase consumer products and services. Figure 2.3 indicates the *per capita* disposable income in this regard of South African consumers according to the nine provinces as calculated in 1994.

FIGURE 2.3 **THE *PER CAPITA* DISPOSABLE INCOME OF SOUTH AFRICAN CONSUMERS ACCORDING TO PROVINCE**

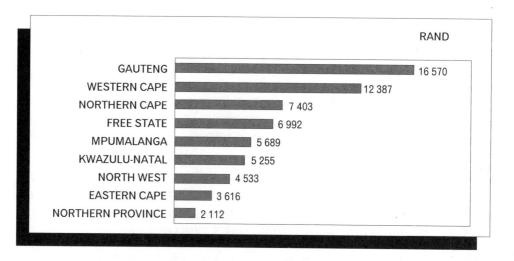

Source: Bureau for Market Research: Personal disposable income of South Africa by population groups and districts, 1985 - 1994.

Only two of the main characteristics of the consumer market, the number of consumers and the buying power of consumers are mentioned above. Numerous other characteristics such as language, age structure, gender distribution, marital status, family size, and literacy influence the spending patterns of the consumer market.

The consumer market can also be grouped into **durable products** (furniture, household appliances and motorcars), **semi-durable products** (clothing, shoes and car tyres) and **non-durable products** (food and tobacco), and **services** (insurance, rent and communication).

This classification enables marketing management to analyse specific segments of the market.

■ **Industrial markets** are markets in which manufacturing organisations buy products and services for their own consumption and/or use in the production of further products or services. This expenditure by the industrial market therefore involves capital goods (machinery, plant and heavy equipment), investment and inventory, and the consumption of raw materials.

■ **Government markets** in South Africa refer to purchases by the general government and the nine provinces and local authorities. The marketing of products and services in industrial and government markets differs from that in the consumer market.

■ **Resale markets** refer to businesses that purchase products and services in order to resell at a profit. This entails trade in a particular country or area and refers, among other things, to wholesale, retail and the liquor trade.

■ **International markets** refer to foreign buyers, and include consumers, manufacturers, resellers and government. Table 2.4 reflects statistics regarding South Africa's exports and imports. Note the positive trade balance for this period.

The preceding discussion of the different markets shows why the market environment is such an important component of the environment for marketing management. Without a continuous study and analysis of this component, marketing management cannot succeed.

### TABLE 2.4 International trade dimensions of South Africa

| INDICATOR | 1992 | 1993 | 1994 | 1995 | 1996 |
|---|---|---|---|---|---|
| EXPORTS (R billion) | 68,4 | 79,0 | 88,6 | 103,8 | 125,1 |
| IMPORTS (R billion) | 51,9 | 59,9 | 76,3 | 98,0 | 116,3 |
| TRADE BALANCE (R billion) | 16,5 | 19,1 | 12,4 | 5,9 | 8,8 |

Source: http://www. mbendi.co.za/land/sa–key.htm

In addition to consumers, who form markets, marketing management should keep abreast of the other components of the market environment.

© Juta

## 2.5.2 Competitors[4]

The contemporary business organisation in the West operates within a market economy and is characterised by competition in the market environment. This means that every business trying to sell a product or service in the market environment is constantly faced with competitors who often determine how much of a given product can be marketed and at what price. Moreover, businesses compete for a share in the market for their product, and they also compete with other businesses for labour, capital, entrepreneurship and material.

As a variable in the market environment, **competition** can be defined as *a situation in the market environment in which several businesses with more or less the same products or services compete for the support of the same consumers.* The result of this competition is that the market mechanism keeps excessive profits in check, acts as an incentive to higher productivity and encourages technological innovation. However, although the consumers benefit from competition, it is nevertheless a variable that management has to take into account in its entry into the operations in the market.

In its assessment of competition, marketing management must bear in mind that the nature and intensity of competition in a particular market environment are determined by five factors:

1. The possibility of new entrants or departures (competitors).
2. The bargaining power of clients and consumers.
3. The bargaining power of suppliers.
4. The availability or even lack of substitute products or services.
5. The number of existing competitors.

Figure 2.4 illustrates the five forces responsible for competition in a particular industry. The collective strength of these five forces determines the competitiveness in the industry and therefore the profitability of the industry. Competition varies from intense, in industries such as tyres and retailing, to moderate in mining and cold-drinks. The weaker the five forces, the better the chances are of success. In spite of the collective strength of the five forces, marketing management still has the task of finding a position in the industry where the business can best defend itself against these forces.

The alternative would be for marketing management to create a position in which the business could influence these forces in its favour. Market segmentation and positioning are discussed in greater detail in chapter 5. Continuous scanning of the competition provides the basis for the development of the marketing strategy. It emphasises the critical strengths and weaknesses of the business, gives an indication of the positioning decisions which must be taken, singles out the areas where strategic changes can contribute the highest returns, and focuses on industry trends in terms of opportunities and threats.

## FIGURE 2.4 COMPETITIVE FORCES IN AN INDUSTRY

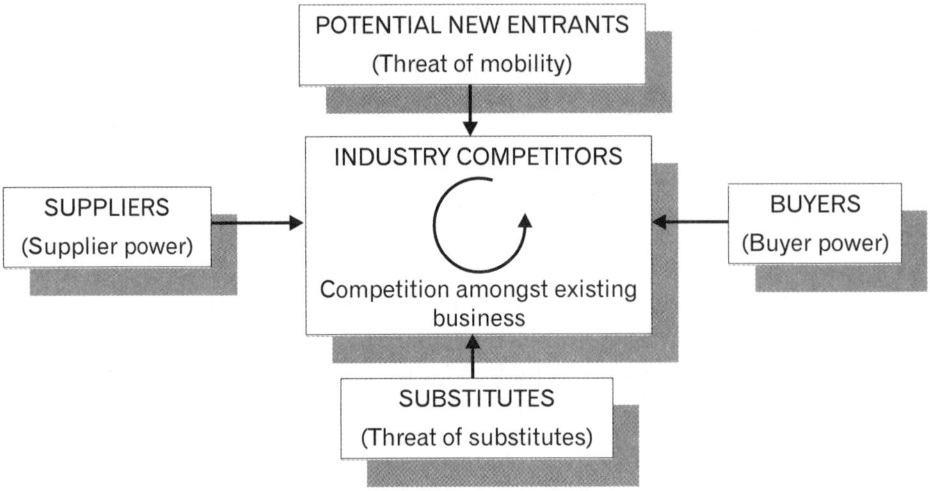

Source: Porter, ME. 1985. Competitive Advantage: Creating and sustaining superior performance. Quoted in Kotler, P. 1997. *Marketing management: analysis, planning, implementation and control.* Engelwood Cliffs, NJ. Prentice Hall, p 229.

### 2.5.3 Intermediaries

Besides consumers and competitors in the market environment, intermediaries also play a vital role in bridging the gap or distance between the manufacturer and the consumer.

By bridging this gap; place, time, and ownership utility are created. Intermediaries are wholesalers and retailers, commercial agents and brokers and, in the Third World, even spaza stores. Among all these intermediaries there are also financial intermediaries such as banks and insurers who, from a financial angle, are also involved in the transfer of products and services.

Decision making by marketing management regarding intermediaries is complicated by the following:

- The dynamic and ever-changing nature of intermediaries. New trends in turnover or consumption are responsible for the development of new types of intermediaries. Examples of contemporary South African trends in this regard are extended shopping hours, the power shift from the manufacturer to large retailer because of bar-coding, and no-name brands, increasing advertising by shopping centres themselves, the growing importance of the black retailer in black residential areas and the increase in the number of franchises, spaza stores and informal retailers such as hawkers. The growth of E-commerce in South Africa poses drastic changes to the structure of competition between intermediaries.

- Decisions about intermediaries means the formation of long-term alliances. This may have certain implications for the marketing strategy. Thus the power of large retailers may have specific implications for price and advertising decisions, and product diversification is dependent on the capacity of intermediaries.

The new trends among intermediaries offer challenges for marketing management, but certain trends can also imply threats.

## 2.5.4 Suppliers

An enterprise is not concerned only with marketing its product but also requires inputs from the market environment. These inputs are primarily material, including raw materials, equipment, energy, capital and labour, which are provided by suppliers. From a marketing perspective, the purchase of products for resale is a critical input on the part of suppliers. When it is realised that about sixty cents (percent) in every rand paid out by the business is spent on purchases from suppliers, the importance thereof as a variable in the market environment becomes clear. If a business cannot obtain the necessary inputs of the required quality in the right quantity and at the right price for the achievement of its objectives, it cannot hope to achieve success in a competitive market environment.

In the case of **materials**, practically every business, whether it is in manufacturing, trading or contracting, depends on regular supplies. As in the case of raw materials, there are suppliers of **capital**, an input upon which the business is dependent for its survival.

Banks, building societies and shareholders are such suppliers. Small organisations, in particular, often find it extremely difficult to attract the necessary capital.

---

**MICROLENDING – A SUPPLIER OF FINANCE THAT NOBODY LOVES!**

Microlending, described as the lending of money to the lower end of the loan market, is growing rapidly in South Africa. This is due to the apparent lack of interest by the big banks in this segment of the population. The exact turnover of the micro-lending industry is difficult to determine but is estimated between R10 billion and R15 billion per year. There are believed to be more than 30 000 micro-lending outlets in South Africa lending money at high interest rates to people who cannot otherwise get credit. This is due to a lack of collateral, high risk or a need for only small amounts that banks do not find profitable to lend. These micro-lenders form a bridge in providing a necessary service to the unbanked masses at the lower end of the South African market.

---

Source: Finance Week 19 March 1999, pp 10–11.

## 2.5.5 Opportunities and threats in the market environment

The changes brought about in the market environment by variables and their interactions, and the trends that constantly develop in the macro-environment, can ultimately be classified into two groups: those that offer an opportunity and those that pose a threat.

An *opportunity* may be defined as a *favourable condition or tendency in the market environment which can be utilised to the benefit of the organisation by means of a deliberate management effort.* It should, however, be clearly understood that the possibilities inherent in an opportunity always have to be assessed against the background of the business's resources and capabilities. Without the necessary capacities and resources, an opportunity cannot be properly utilised. The success of a business in making good use of an opportunity therefore depends upon its ability to satisfy the requirement for success in that particular market.

In contrast to the environmental opportunity, an environmental *threat* may be defined as *an unfavourable condition or tendency in the market environment that can, in the absence of a deliberate effort by management lead to the failure of the business, its product or its service.*

In view of the constant changes in the market environment, it is the duty of management to identify such threats, both actual and potential, and to develop a counter-strategy or contingency strategy to meet them.

### 2.5.6 The market environment – determining opportunities and threats

The market environment entails an interaction between a business and its suppliers, consumers, and competitors with alternative marketing offerings. The interaction can result in opportunities or threats to a business, and marketing management must be aware of trends in the market environment so management can utilise opportunities profitably and avoid threats in good time. For this purpose, environmental scanning, marketing research and information management are the proper instruments.

## 2.6   THE  MACRO-ENVIRONMENT

### 2.6.1 The composition of the macro-environment

Apart from the market environment, which has a direct effect on the fortunes of a business, a wider macro-environment exists, containing variables that directly or indirectly exert an influence on the business and its market environment. These variables constitute those uncontrollable forces in the environment that are sometimes referred to as *megatrends*. As can be seen from Figure 2.2, the contemporary literature on management divides the macro-environment into six variables, namely technological, economic, social, physical, institutional or political, and international variables (or sub-environments). The technological environment is responsible for the rate of innovation and change. The economic environment involves factors such as inflation, recessions and exchange rates and the monetary and fiscal policies that influence the welfare of the business and its community. The social environment concerns the individual's way of life, customs and standards formed by his or her culture and these also make certain demands on the business. The physical environment comprises natural resources as well as the improvements made by people, for example, roads and bridges, mineral wealth and flora and fauna. The institutional environment embraces the government with its political involvement and legislation as the main components; and, finally, the international environment concerns local and foreign political trends and events that influence organisations and the market environment.

## 2.6.2 The technological environment

Scientists estimate the age of the earth to be five billion years and the existence of people 250 000 years. History dates back approximately 5 000 years. The products which exist today, excluding a few basic products, were developed during the past 60 years. And the latest products which have already become indispensable to modern society, such as laser surgery, robotics, silicon protein molecules, organ transplants and fibre optics, and about 80% of today's medicines are the products of the last ten years! This tremendous environmental change is largely a manifestation of technological innovation, a process which enlarges the capabilities of mankind.

Technological innovation originates in research and development by business as well as the state, and results not only in new machinery or products but also new processes, methods, and even new approaches to management that bring about change in the environment. Even the social and institutional progress in a country and the structures it possesses relate to technology. Technological innovation also affects other environmental variables. The economic growth rate is influenced by the number of new inventions as well as social change, for example, the appearance of a new product such as television brings about a revolution in people's way of life. These variables in turn influence technology, and so the process of innovation and change is repeated.

Every new technological development or innovation creates opportunities and threats in the environment. Television was a threat to films and newspapers, but at the same time presented opportunities for instant meals, satellite communication and the advertising industry. The opportunities created by computers in banking, manufacturing, transport and practically every industry are innumerable. The exhibit illustrates the use of the Internet as a technology revolution.

Moreover, technological or scientific innovation often has unpredictable consequences: the contraceptive pill meant smaller families, more women at work, and therefore more disposable income to spend on holidays and luxury articles, which would previously not have been possible. The most outstanding characteristic of technological innovation is probably the fact that it constantly accelerates the rate of change.

Marketing management has a threefold involvement in the process of technological innovation and change. **Firstly**, it promotes technological innovation when it identifies new consumer needs and when it influences technology in such a way that it leads to the satisfaction of those consumer needs. **Secondly**, it distributes technological innovation throughout society – that is, marketing tracks down new inventions and then develops and commercialises them.

**Thirdly**, marketing management is involved in scanning technological progress and the opportunities and threats that it poses for the business.

## THE INTERNET BUSINESS - CLICK TILL YOU DROP!

The Internet technological revolution will reshape the way everyone does business. Before the first decade of the new century is out, the Internet will be a standard feature in the lives of not only every businessperson, but it will pervade into every consumer's personal life. Today, one can buy just about anything on the Internet, from household groceries and luxury goods to computers and motorcars.

The Internet has already resulted in some front-line businesses changing the way in which they are doing their business.

The entire home salesforce of the 230 year-old Encyclopaedia Britannica, in the UK, Germany and North America were dismissed. At $ 8.50 a month for browsing rights, the expenditure on the Internet is much less than it would be owning a $ 1 250, 32-volume set of books. Children are much more inclined to obtain their information online or from a CD-ROM.

In 1988, 25% of all the online users in the USA shopped on the Internet with an estimated 16 million shoppers worldwide shopping on the Internet. Estimated online revenues per industry are as follows:

| | |
|---|---|
| Travel $ 2 091 million | PC Hardware $ 1 816 million |
| Groceries $ 1 816 million | Gifts/flowers $ 219 million |
| Books $ 216 million | PC Software $ 173 million |
| Tickets $ 127 million | Music $ 81 million |
| Clothing $ 71 million | |

Source: Time, 3 August 1998, pp 40–45.

Marketing management therefore has a significant task to perform in managing the transition to a new technology because technological innovation can have a fast and drastic effect on a product or industry. A case in point is the detrimental influence of quartz watches on the manufacturing of conventional watches previously referred to. However, this does not mean that a certain technological innovation will render the older technology obsolete. Various observations have been made in this regard:

- A new technological advancement does not necessarily smother an old technology, but can even stimulate its growth because the threatened organisations improve their old technologies. Safety razor sales, for example, have actually increased 800% since the advent of the electric razor.

- In most cases, firms involved in the old technology have a substantial amount of time to react to the new technology.

- It is relatively difficult to predict the outcome of a new technology, and it tends to create new markets instead of encroaching on existing ones. For example, throw-away ballpoint pens created new markets without killing the market for refillable ballpoint pens.

- A further characteristic that marketing management should bear in mind is that technological innovations are unlimited and that they continuously affect the environment. Table 2.5 illustrates possible technological innovations which can entail endless possibilities and threats for the marketer in the near future.

In scanning the technological environment, marketing management must keep in mind the maturity of an existing technology, and its possible replacement with a new one. Technological innovation is especially possible when:

- the physical boundaries of an existing technology are reached;

- research and development in a certain area become uneconomical; and

- competitors start to experiment with expensive and risky technology.

Technological progress, therefore, affects the business as a whole, including its product, life cycle, supply of materials, production processes, management approach, and ultimately its position in the market.

Hence marketing management should be increasingly alert to technological changes.

## TABLE 2.5  Promising products and services through technological innovation

- Practical solar energy.

- Cancer cures.

- Car navigation systems.

- Electronic anaesthetic for pain-killing.

- Commercial space shuttle.

- Non-fattening, tasty, nutritious foods.

- Electric cars.

- Voice- and gesture-controlled computers.

Source: Kotler, P and Armstrong, G. 1996. *Principles of marketing*. 7th edition. Englewood Cliffs, NJ: Prentice Hall, p 84.

### 2.6.3  The economic environment

After technology, which is primarily responsible for change in the environment, follows the economy, which is influenced by technology, politics, and the social and international environments, while it in turn also asserts some influence on these variables. These cross-influences cause ongoing change in the economic growth rate, levels of employment, consumer income, the inflation rate and the general state of the economy, which is indicated by either prosperity or adversity. Ultimately, these economic forces will have implications for the business and marketing management. The main interfaces between the economic environment and the business are the economic growth rate, consumer income, inflation, monetary and fiscal policy and fluctuations in these magnitudes.

The economic well-being of a community is measured by the range and number of products and services produced. Expressed in financial terms, this standard is equivalent to the gross domestic product – that is, *the total value of finished products and services produced within the borders of a country during a given period, usually a year*.

During the thirty years after the Second World War, the average real growth of the South African GDP was about 4,7% per annum, after which, from 1970 to 1988, it declined to an average annual rate of 2,8%, and thereafter even to lower levels. The GDP for 1996 was 3,1%, for 1997 it dropped to 1,7%, whilst the GPD for 1998 is estimated to be 0%

The fact that South Africa's population growth of 2,5% is increasing faster than its economic growth rate means that the standard of living of its inhabitants has declined even further. This trend of impoverishment is exacerbated by an above average influx of immigrants from neighbouring states and rising unemployment figures.

Table 2.6 shows the 1996 census figures depicting the average individual income per employed person and unemployment figures per province. Gauteng is the richest province and also is the home of more than half of the wealthiest people in South Africa. Of the 20 000 people who earn more than R360 000 per year, close to 50% live in Gauteng. The Northern Province has the lowest average individual income among the employed and the second highest unemployment rate (46%).

The structural changes in the incomes of different consumer groups are of great importance to marketing management, since they give rise to changing spending patterns with regard to products and services such as food, clothing, housing and insurance.

## TABLE 2.6  Average individual income per person and the unemployment rate of South Africans in 1996

| PROVINCE | AVERAGE INDIVIDUAL INCOME PER EMPLOYED PERSON PER YEAR | UNEMPLOYMENT RATE PER PROVINCE |
|---|---|---|
| EASTERN CAPE | R 22 100 | 49% |
| FREE STATE | R 18 500 | 30% |
| GAUTENG | R 33 500 | 28% |
| KWAZULU-NATAL | R 24 300 | 39% |
| MPUMALANGA | R 19 900 | 33% |
| NORTHERN CAPE | R 20 100 | 29% |
| NORTHERN PROVINCE | R 17 900 | 46% |
| NORTH WEST | R 18 900 | 38% |
| WESTERN CAPE | R 28 900 | 18% |

Source: Sunday Times, 25 October 1998, p 5.

Although the economic growth rate has a decisive effect on marketing management, it is the correct gauging of the upswing and downswing phases of the economy that has a significant influence on marketing strategy. If an organisation is expecting a recession, it can benefit by reducing inventory timeously because its stocks could be difficult to sell, by maintaining a state of liquidity to avoid the high cost of interest or by postponing any ideas of expansion indefinitely. In the case of an upswing, a sound strategy would be to build up sufficient inventory in good time and carry out whatever expansion is necessary to meet increased demand.

Inflation, like growth, is an economic variable that influences the decisions made by management. An inflation rate of more than 10% has been a regular phenomenon since the 1970s. The average inflation rate has declined since 1993 with an inflation rate of below 10% from 1993 onwards. South Africa's inflation rate is, however, still higher than her main trading partners. Hence it is the task of management to constantly study the effect of inflation on products and services, or rather the implications thereof on the market strategy.

The effects of inflation on the business are profound. For example, it causes phantom profit, while making inroads on capital; it makes cost accounting and the financing of credit difficult. It forces the industrial buyer to build up supplies, while consumers adjust their behaviour to take account of keener price competition, increasing the importance of functionalism and buying early in anticipation of price rises – which often leads to another round of inflationary demand. Inflationary pressures in South Africa are expected to remain reasonably high for the next ten years, the most pressure coming from the wage demands of trade unions. In the long term this will result in new consumer values, spending and impoverishment. However, new values also mean new opportunities and new markets.

Another economic variable affecting a business and its market environment is the government's monetary policy, in accordance with which the money supply, interest rates and the position of a country's monetary unit relative to the disturbances that other countries' monetary units can cause in the environment. Fiscal policy affects both the business and the consumer through taxation rates and tax reforms.

These economic trends which were briefly discussed as a few examples of economic change, demand a constant awareness by marketing management and regular consideration of the mission and strategy of the business.

## 2.6.4 The social environment

The environmental variable probably most subject to the influence of other variables, especially technology and the economy, is social change. Precisely because it affects management indirectly through people as consumers and employees, the ultimate effect of social change on the strategy of a business should not be underestimated.

People are the products of their community: as members of a particular community they accept and assimilate its language, its values, its faith, expectations, laws and customs. This culture, the sum total of the way of life of a group of people influences the individual's way of life. Thus consumption cannot be explained solely in economic terms – the effects of culture and social change must also be considered. However, culture is not static, but over time changes a community's values, expectations, lifestyle and customs.

The culture of a particular country is also not completely homogeneous. There are also many subcultures based on such things as nationality, religion, population group or geographic area, each of which entails a distinctive change in the environment with further implications for management.

> ### CHANGES IN THE USE OF THE ENGLISH LANGUAGE
>
> In Shakespeare's time only 150 000 of the 450 000 words now part of the English language existed. Were he alive today, he would understand only five words out of nine.

The business stands at the centre of social change. On the one hand, it contributes to social change, while, on the other, it should constantly be aware of the major influences of social currents on itself. We shall now briefly examine a few observable social trends. Demographic change, that is, change in the growth and the composition of populations, is probably the social variable that causes the most change in the market by altering people's way of life.

In this regard, Western societies are characterised by falling population growth rates and shrinking families, with the emphasis on smaller consumer units.

There are growing numbers of one-person households, and consequently there is a growing demand for services. There is a growing population of ageing and more affluent people and families over the age of 65 who create special marketing opportunities. There are also increasing numbers of one-parent families, with definite implications for the market and for the social responsibilities of the business.

In contrast to the above, developing communities are characterised by high population growth rates, of which the largest percentage are under the age of 18, declining standards of living with a waning demand for basic consumer goods and no demand for services. Table 2.7 represents the growth rate of the South African population to the year 2011.

## TABLE 2.7  Annual population increases and growth rates of the South African population

| Population group | 1991-1996 | 1996-2001 | 2001-2006 | 2006-2011 |
|---|---|---|---|---|
| Asians | 13 600 | 13 000 | 10 800 | 8 100 |
| % | 1,34 | 1,20 | 0,95 | 0,68 |
| Blacks | 713 600 | 757 100 | 749 500 | 700 300 |
| % | 2,40 | 2,26 | 2,01 | 1,71 |
| Coloureds | 48 700 | 45 500 | 39 500 | 31 700 |
| % | 1,44 | 1,26 | 1,03 | 0,79 |
| Whites | 34 800 | 28 200 | 19 400 | 9 700 |
| % | 0,68 | 0,53 | 0,36 | 0,18 |
| Total | 810 700 | 843 800 | 819 200 | 749 800 |
| % | 2,06 | 1,94 | 1,72 | 1,45 |

Source: Bureau for Market Research. 1993. A projection of the South African population, 1991–2011. Research report No. 196. UNISA, p 5.

The table shows an expected declining growth rate for all four groups. The expectation is that the population is going to increase to about 54 million by the year 2011, whereafter the growth rate of black consumers will decline from 2,40% per annum to 1,71% per annum.

Whites, whose growth rate is 0,68% per annum, will reach an almost zero growth rate in the year 2011. At present, about 41% of the black population are younger than 14 years of age. Demographic trends that influence the purchase of products and services are the following:

- **Urbanisation**, employment and the ability to provide housing, food and urban services. Less developed countries are characterised by phenomenal growth in urbanisation, increasing unemployment, increasing pollution and the growth of informal settlements, where it is a question of merely satisfying basic needs.

- **The changing population composition** in developed countries provides a significant over-65 market for housing, insurance, health care and tourism. In less developed countries, there is an increasing juvenile segment of the market, with less spending power.

- **The increasing economic power of women** with wider interests outside the home, more expendable income and less time to buy.

- **The increase in the number of households** because of the rise in the divorce rate. Smaller and more households mean a larger market for household equipment, products and services.

Another social variable with clear implications for management is the changing role of women in Western society. As recently as fifteen years ago, 60% of American women believed that a woman's place was in the home. Nowadays, only 22% are of that opinion.

Working women are regarded as the decisive factor in the development of supermarkets, extended shopping hours and take-away meals. With a greater disposable income and less time to buy, they are prepared to pay for convenience.

These developments entail changes in the lives of women and consequently of their families, and also affect their buying patterns by shifting women's shopping hours mostly to weekends and causing women to favour shopping centres catering for practically all their needs. This trend also puts new pressure on management for equal opportunities for women in management and to provide day-care facilities for the children of working mothers. The demand for 'convenience products' affects management particularly.

A further trend that has to be considered is **consumerism**, the social force that protects the consumer by exerting legal, moral, economic and even political pressure on management. This movement is a natural consequence of a better-educated public that resists such things as misleading advertisements, unsafe products, profiteering and other objectionable practices, and presses for the rights of the consumer. These aspects are discussed in chapter 4.

The final aspect of the social environment that merits attention is the pressure society exerts on the business organisation, forcing it to be socially responsible. This means that organisations should act responsibly in the environment in which they operate and constantly consider the consequences of their decisions and actions. In many respects, criticism of the actions of organisations such as misleading advertising, dangerous products, pollution of the environment and exploitation of the consumer are levelled at marketing management, probably because marketing is responsible for providing the ultimate product or service.

### 2.6.5 The physical environment

The physical environment embraces the limited resources from which the business obtains its raw materials, as well as the environment into which it discharges its waste. This has bearing on various forms of pollution. Since the 1960s, there has been growing concern about our natural environment, particularly with regard to a shortage of resources, protest against all forms of pollution and the destruction of the environment by opencast mining, the building of roads and dams, and speculation about whether the theories of Malthus and others regarding the overpopulation of the earth are in fact being confirmed. Business itself has developed an awareness of the physical environment, because this can affect the oganisation in many ways. Certain interfaces that present opportunities as well as threats to the business can be discerned.

- The *first* interface involves a broad range of resources that are becoming increasingly scarce, such as raw materials, energy and foodstuffs. These have certain implications for management. Shortages affect the supply of goods, contribute to inflation and cause severe price rises, and often necessitate different methods of manufacturing and a reorientation of marketing thought in an effort to find substitutes for unobtainable products.

- The *second* interface is the increasing cost of energy, which also influences the environment with consequent opportunities and threats for the business. The rise in the price of oil, from $2 a barrel in 1970 to $34 in 1982, set in motion a frantic search for alternative sources of energy. Coal was once again in great demand, so that South Africa became second only to Poland as a coal exporter.

Research on solar, wind and nuclear power was intensified, and the costs of nuclear power were studied.

South Africa is fairly rich in energy sources, with 10% of the world's coal reserves, 18% of the Western world's uranium reserves, the Sasol plants and some gas and oil off the southern Cape coast.

■ The **third** interface between the business and its physical environment is the growing cost of urban pollution to the community in terms of a destroyed environment. The expense of fighting pollution and the laws that business have to obey in this regard are also important here. However, opportunities also present themselves in the form of recycling and new methods of manufacturing and packaging products in order to reduce pollution to the minimum.

---

### WORLD'S NATURAL WEALTH DWINDLING

A third of the world's natural resources have been consumed in the 25 years ending in 1995. The decline is especially concentrated on freshwater lakes, rivers and wetlands. Freshwater ecosystems were disappearing at a rate of 6% a year and had halved in number between 1970 and 1995.

The world's natural forest cover is falling by 0,5% per year for a total loss of 10% between 1970 and 1995. In world consumption since 1960, grain and fish consumption more than doubled and wood and freshwater consumption had increased one and a half times. Cement consumption, a measure of urban expansion, had more that quadrupled since 1960. Carbon dioxide emissions have also increased by almost three times in the same period.

---

Source: Business Day, 2 October 1998, p 8.

■ The **fourth** interface between the business and the physical environment is the field of environmentalism, which may be defined as **an organised movement of citizens and government institutions in defence of the natural environment**. Although the responsibility for a well-ordered ecology cannot be said to rest entirely with business organisations, they do make their mark on the ecology, for example by way of advertising boards, packaging materials such as beer cans, soft-drink bottles and a variety of paper containers, all of which cause pollution, not to mention the marketing of products that are detrimental to people and the natural environment, as the exhibit shows.

## DESTRUCTION OF THE ECOLOGY

The weedkillers used by maize farmers to spray their crops, in North West province particularly, constitute only one of many examples. They take years to break down chemically, and they adhere to the soil particles. The wind blows these polluted grains of sand on to blades of grass and the leaves of trees, and with the first showers the poisons are washed down and absorbed through the roots, killing off the flora. A further ecological objection is that excessive advertising and aggressive marketing give rise to greatly increased demand, leading to the plundering of sometimes scarce natural resources.

Management should respond timeously by taking steps to limit any harmful effects on the community as far as possible. If management does not show a decent sense of responsibility, they should not be surprised if hostile attitudes develop – attitudes that may threaten the very survival of the business. Thus the packaging industry is developing containers to minimise pollution, the soap industry is conducting research on less harmful chemicals, and the motor industry is being compelled by legislation to develop alternative energy resources and to design exhaust systems that will minimise pollution.

### 2.6.6 The politico-governmental environment

Management decisions are continually affected by a country's politics, especially the political pressures exerted by the government and its institutions in the business environment. As a component of the macro-environment, government affects the business environment and the business primarily as a regulating institution. By promulgating the enforcing legislation, it creates order by means of political measures, steering agricultural and economic policy in a particular direction. The policy of the South African government is based on maintaining the free-market system, private ownership, freedom of vocation and public condemnation of inequality, while the democratisation of the economy and public service are in full swing.

Hence the government intervenes in the local market on a large scale by means of the annual budget, taxation, import control or lack thereof, promotion of exports, import tariffs to protect certain industries against excessive foreign competition, price control for certain goods and services, health regulation, as well as incentives and other measures to encourage development in a specific direction.

BLACK ECONOMIC EMPOWERMENT IN SOUTH AFRICA

It is the government's policy to actively promote a more equitable distribution of wealth in a free market context by supporting and favouring the economic empowerment of people from historically disadvantaged communities in the grant of State tenders and procurement contracts, licences (for example, casino, radio and cellular licences) and financial and other assistance by the State to businesses. Joint ventures with historically disadvantaged communities and entities controlled by them have accordingly become commonplace. The private sector has also been involved in empowerment transactions and some major corporations have emerged which are controlled by historically disadvantaged people.

Source: http://www.mbendi.co.za/werksmns/SABuso1.htm.

The government also influences the market both internally and externally – internally through government investment and externally through its political policy, which may determine the acceptability or otherwise of South Africa for foreign investors. Whenever the government acts as a producer, as in the case of numerous government organisations, it competes with private business for labour, raw material and capital.

Privatisation, which occurs at a rather sluggish rate in South Africa, and which lacks credibility because of the growth rate in the public service workforce, can also create opportunities and threats. Since 1979, the British government has sold 40% of its assets at a value of some R40 billion to nine million private investors.

China is also moving in a direction of a free-market system and through privatisation has maintained a GDP and growth rate of 10% per annum for the past eight years. Russia is also moving in the direction of privatisation, which means that in the future large consumer markets will probably be found in the East with China the emerging giant for the next millenium.

To an increasing extent, it is the task of management to study the numerous and often complex activities, legislation and measures of government as well as political trends to determine in good time their influence on the profitable survival of the business.

## 2.6.7  The international environment

While each of the above environmental factors to a greater or lesser extent influences the business environment of each organisation, the situation is rendered even more complex with more opportunities and threats when an international dimension is added to each of the environmental factors. Businesses that operate internationally find themselves in a far more complex business environment because every country has its own unique environmental factors, with its own technology, culture, laws, politics, markets and competitiveness, which are different from those of other countries.

International and multinational organisations in particular are susceptible to all sorts of international currents.

The new economic order which is taking shape throughout the world is the increasing globalisation of the world economy. South African marketers should be able to find new opportunities now that South Africa has been readmitted to the international economic community.

Nowadays, nations are also more dependent than ever on each other's technologies, economics, politics and raw material, so that the developments in these fields inevitably influence the decisions of management. Developing countries depend on technology imported from developed countries for their self-development. Inventions are excellent export products that offer opportunities, especially in the light of South Africa's expertise in mining, exploration of minerals, oil-from-coal technology and veterinary science.

The influence of international economic and political developments on local business, particularly in view of their closely interrelated nature, is multiple, and South African managers are only too aware of the extent to which international influences are exacerbated by our domestic political problems.

## 2.6.8  Dynamic environment

In a free-market system, a business exists in a dynamic environment in which technological innovation, economic fluctuations, changing communities and lifestyles, as well as political change continually alter the environment and ultimately affect it.

An insight into and understanding of trends and events in the environment and an ability to foresee the implications thereof for decision making are becoming increasingly important for management since past experience in a rapidly changing environment is often of little help in solving new problems that confront management, and mere expansion of issues that largely determine the direction in which the business will develop are also necessary for decision making in order to maximise profitability. This knowledge requires environmental scanning that enables management to identify threats and demands in the environment timeously and, wherever possible, to turn them into opportunities.

## 2.7  METHODS OF ENVIRONMENTAL SCANNING

The degree to which the environment influences the management of a business depends largely on the type of business and the objectives it intends achieving. Moreover, environmental influences differ from one management function to the next and even at different levels of management in an organisation. As such, the importance, scope and method of environmental scanning – that is, the process dealing with the measurement, projection and evaluation of change in the different environmental variables – differs from one business to the next.

The importance of environmental scanning is clear from the following points:

■ The environment is continually changing, so that purposeful scanning by management is necessary to keep abreast of change.

■ Scanning is necessary to determine which factors in the environment pose a threat to the business's present goals and strategy.

■ Scanning is also necessary to determine which factors in the environment present opportunities for the more effective attainment of goals by modifying present strategy.

■ Businesses that scan the environment systematically are more successful than those that do not.

The scope of environmental scanning is determined by the following factors:

■ The nature of the environment within which the business operates and the demands made by the environment on the business. The more unstable the environment and the more sensitive the business is to change, the more comprehensive the scanning has to be. Increasing instability usually means greater risk for the business.

■ Managers nowadays should constantly bear in mind the basic relationships between the business and its environment. The importance or otherwise of any one or more of these relationships for management will affect the scope of environmental scanning.

■ The source and scope of change will also influence the extent of meaningful environmental scanning. The impact of change is rarely so compartmentalised that it influences only one or two areas of an organisation. Change has an interactive and dynamic effect on various facets of the business.

The method of environmental scanning is a much-debated subject, and the following possible approaches can be followed:

■ The most elementary basis for environmental scanning is *to keep abreast of the relevant secondary or published information obtainable from a vast wealth of sources*, such as the media, own data, professional publications, financial journals, statistics, associates in other organisations, banks, research institutions and even employees. Such information may be added to the management information system of the organisation.

■ A more advanced basis for scanning would be the *addition of primary information or special studies on particular aspects of the environment*. Such studies can be carried out by members or the organisation's own staff or by outside consultants.

■ A far more advanced basis is the *establishment of a unit within the organisation which scans a wide range of environmental factors and makes forecasts about specific variables*. Examples here are the *economic predictions* made by economists using a number of models, market and competition assessments by market researchers, and technological predictions by industrial analysts. Such a scanning unit is usually located in the planning department of top management and has its own staff.

The question that now arises is how this collected environmental information can be brought to the attention of the appropriate manager. There are many different opinions about this, the most popular approach being that environmental information forms the basis of strategic planning undertaken by top management.

## SUMMARY

The business and the community it serves are not self-sufficient and closed entities but depend on each other for survival. Together they form a complex, dynamic business or marketing environment in which changes in the environmental variables continually determine the prosperity or otherwise of the business. Since these variables are more often than not beyond the control of the organisation, it is the task of management to adapt constantly to change. Sometimes management operates proactively – in other words, management takes the lead and anticipates events – thereby augmenting change.

Knowledge of a changing environment through sustained environmental scanning is a prerequisite for taking advantage of opportunities and averting threats. Environmental scanning is discussed in chapter 3, which deals with marketing research.

## REFERENCES

1. Based on Cronje; GJ de J, Du Toit, GS; Mol, AJ; Van Reenen, MJ, and Motlatla (eds).1994. *Inleiding tot die bestuurswese*. Johannesburg: Southern, Chapter 3.

2. Pearce, JA and Robinson, RB. 1988. *Formulation and implementation of competitive strategy*. Homewood, Ill; Richard D Irwin Inc, p 202.

3. Vasconcellos e Sa', J. 1988. The impact of key success factors on company performance. *Long-range planning*. Vol 21, pp 56 – 64.

4. Kotler, P. 1997. *Marketing management: analysis, planning, implementation and control*. Englewood Cliffs, NJ: Prentice Hall, p 229.

# CHAPTER 3

--------------------------------| MARKETING RESEARCH

## 3.1  INTRODUCTION

Whether competing in local markets or foreign markets, a company's ability to gather and monitor marketing information keeps it on track. In fact, information is the engine that drives today's global marketplace. Companies succeed by knowing what consumers want, when they want it, and where they want it – and by knowing what competing companies are doing about it. A sophisticated database of marketing information is a vital component in the strategy of cutting-edge companies that pull ahead and stay ahead in the race for customers.

### SUCCESSFUL COMPANIES RELY ON INFORMATION

Companies such as General Motors, McDonald's and Mercedes-Benz have long, successful marketing histories. Why are these companies so successful? In each case, it is because the marketers have correctly 'heard' the consumers' wants and needs, and conceived a product (or service), price, promotion and distribution method that satisfied those wants and needs.

Mercedes-Benz, for example, monitors luxury car markets around the world. The company relies on consumer research and marketing information from many sources to keep on top of what product benefits, features and services customers all over the world desire and will accept. Mercedes-Benz stays out in front of the highly competitive market by finding out what it takes to tempt consumers into spending up to R600 000 for their high-quality driving machines.

Some information about consumers and conditions in the marketplace is easy to acquire. At other times marketers need to conduct in-depth research to make informed marketing decisions.

By keeping a sharp eye on day-to-day customer activity, for example, marketing managers can respond very quickly to changes in consumers' needs and buying patterns that mean the difference between the success and failure of marketing plans.

Marketing researchers have begun to use the Internet for a variety of marketing research purposes. The use of the Internet has grown and continues to grow at a staggering rate. The Internet impacts the marketing research industry in various ways: it can virtually replace libraries and various printed materials as sources of secondary data; it serves as a vehicle for data collection; it aids in project management; it can be used to distribute reports; and team members working on a project can use it to communicate with each other.

## RESEARCH REPORTS ON THE INTERNET

Research reports can be published to the Web directly from programs such as PowerPoint and all the latest versions of leading word processing, spreadsheets, and presentation software packages. This means that results are available worldwide almost instantly. Reports can be searched for content of interest using the same Web browser used to view the report itself.

In this chapter, we look at the kinds of information marketers need and how they gather and use that information to develop marketing strategies that make a difference. In this discussion, we focus on the marketing information system, marketing research, and market potential and sales forecasting.

## LEARNING OUTCOMES

At the end of this chapter you will be able to:

- highlight the role of marketing research in decision making;
- explain the components of the marketing information system;
- explain and illustrate the steps in the marketing research process;
- refer throughout to the important role of the Internet in marketing research; and
- give an overview of market potential and sales forecasting, a specific element of marketing information.

## 3.2   THE ROLE OF MARKETING RESEARCH IN DECISION MAKING

### 3.2.1 The value of marketing information

Marketing research can be defined as '. . . *the process of designing, gathering, analysing and reporting information that may be used to solve a specific marketing problem*'.[1] The importance of the role of marketing research is reflected in this definition since it specifies the ways that the information provided by marketing research may be used.

The main role of marketing research is to provide information that facilitates marketing decisions.[2]   We know that marketing is the '*performance of all activities necessary for the conception, pricing, promotion and distribution of ideas, goods and services to create exchanges that satisfy individual and organisational objectives*'. The potential for *exchange* exists when there are at least two parties and each has something of potential value to the other. Now the question arises, 'How do marketing managers attempt to stimulate exchange?' They follow the 'right' principle: they attempt to get the right goods and services to the right people at the right place at the right time at the right price using the right promotion techniques. In order to make the 'right' decisions, management must have timely decision-making information, and marketing research is a primary channel for providing that information.

In terms of the consumer orientation principle of the marketing concept, companies strive to identify the group of people most likely to buy their product (the target market) and produce goods or services that will meet the needs of the target customers most effectively. But how does a company know what consumers' needs and wants are? Obviously marketers must have information about consumers' needs and wants if they are truly to endorse the marketing concept. Identifying target market needs and market opportunities is the task of marketing research.

Quality and customer satisfaction have become the key competitive weapons of the late 1990s.[3] Few organisations will prosper in today's environment without a focus on quality and customer satisfaction. The key to quality and customer satisfaction is marketing research – it is the mechanism that enables companies to determine what types and forms of quality are important to the target market.

Customer satisfaction and quality lead to customer retention. The ability to retain customers is based upon an intimate understanding of their needs. This knowledge comes primarily from marketing research.

## CUSTOMER SERVICE AT TOYOTA

Toyota SA realised in the mid-eighties that a shift of focus was needed to satisfy the customers – the concept of customer satisfaction had to be managed and measured. By shifting the focus and educating dealers to see through the customer's eyes, Toyota tried to improve the service experience of customers. The Toyota Touch programme, implemented in the mid-eighties included:

■ Establishing and maintaining a customer-oriented culture.

■ Developing an obsession among staff at Toyota with customers and the satisfaction of their needs.

■ Developing a competitive advantage in terms of customer satisfaction by aiming for a top rating in the SA motor industry.

Toyota succeeded in establishing a competitive advantage in terms of customer service. Its overall rating by customers has increased every year since 1986. In the 1998 Sunday Times/Markinor Top Brands survey, Toyota was rated one of the top ten brands in South Africa, as well as the fifth most admired company in South Africa. The Toyota Touch strategy relies heavily on marketing research in the form of regular surveys.

## BRITISH AIRWAYS: UNDERSTANDING CUSTOMER NEEDS

British Airways research found that most first-class passengers simply wanted to sleep. BA now gives business-class passengers the option of dinner on the ground, before takeoff, in the first-class lounge. Once on board, they can slip into BA pyjamas, put their heads on real pillows, slip under blankets, and then enjoy an interruption-free flight.

Marketing research is also used in decision making about the marketing mix, keeping abreast of changes in the marketing environment, identifying and defining marketing opportunities and problems in an effort to monitor marketing performance and to improve our understanding of the marketing process.

### 3.2.2 Marketing research and the marketing mix

Marketers must also implement plans, called marketing strategies, that actually satisfy consumers' wants and needs. Within the marketing department, a marketing mix, based on the marketing concept, must be created. This mix is the unique blend of the four Ps (product, price, promotion and place) designed to reach a specific group of consumers (target market).[4] What combination of the four Ps will best take advantage of an existing marketing opportunity? This may sound simple, but consider some of the questions that confront marketing managers as they design marketing strategies:

---

**QUESTIONS TO ANSWER IN DESIGNING MARKETING STRATEGIES**

■ Who is the market?

■ How do we segment the market?

■ What are the wants and needs of each segment?

■ How do we measure the size of each market segment?

■ Who are our competitors, and how are they meeting the wants and needs of each segment?

■ Which segment(s) should we target?

■ Which model of a proposed product will best suit the target market?

■ What is the best price?

■ Which promotional method will be the most efficient?

■ How should we distribute the product/service?

---

These questions must be answered. Therefore, marketing managers need objective, accurate and current information in order to develop marketing strategies that will work. Sears, the well-known US retailer, for example, relies heavily on consumer research.

CONSUMER RESEARCH AT SEARS

Sears, a well-known American retailer, identified, through a nationwide research study conducted in 1992, that its best customers for Craftsman tools and Kenmore appliances were women, aged 25 to 50, who do almost all the family shopping. However, when it came to their own needs, women went elsewhere because Sears did not carry much brand name apparel. Cashing in on the campaign to target women, Sears is now launching its 'Circle of Beauty' line of makeup, skin care products and fragrances.

Sears has spent heavily on consumer research, testing everything from names to products and packaging. The result of this turnaround is that Sears went from a $2,9 billion loss in 1992 to a $1,6 billion operating profit during 1993 and 1994.

## 3.2.3 Marketing research and the macro-marketing environment

Even when marketers have the right information to implement an effective marketing strategy, they must be constantly aware of changing environments. A change in the environment may alter the appeal of a marketing strategy to consumers. So, because the environments are constantly changing, marketers' needs for information are never ending. Information about the social and cultural environment, economic environment, political environment and technological environment is of particular importance to marketing management in their decision making.

- *Social and cultural environment*. Changes taking place in the social and cultural environment must be monitored. For example, as the population grows older, companies are developing products and services for the elderly. Several companies are also redesigning their products for the elderly. For instance, computer keyboards have been developed with large type, making them easier for older people to use.

- *The economic environment.* Marketing strategy is also highly dependent on the economic environment. A change in interest rate, for example, can have a significant impact on business. Marketers use marketing research to keep abreast of these changes.

## THE SOUTH AFRICAN SOCIAL ENVIRONMENT[5]

South African business is affected by the following changes in the social environment:

- The narrowing gap in the standards of living of black consumers and white consumers and the rise in literacy among black people.

- The increasing number of one-parent families.

- The black age structure that reflects a much more youthful population, largely urbanised – these impact on demand and consumption patterns.

- Growing urbanisation which resulted, for example, in the advent of the spaza store.

- The changing role of women in our society.

## THE SOUTH AFRICAN ECONOMIC ENVIRONMENT[6]

Important factors in the economic environment which impact on business are:

- The inflation rate (in 1996 it was 7,4%) results in high prices and changes in consumer spending.

- In 1999 we entered a period of recession, signifying increasing unemployment, decreasing purchases and a resultant decline in profit.

- The white household income is six times that of black households.

- Black households have a major share of the market for many individual products such as washing materials, clothing, footwear, cigarettes and tobacco.

- Violence discourages foreign investment and tourism.

- **Political environment**. The political environment, by way of the government, influences society indirectly via its influence on the economy and technology.

The political environment thus influences marketing strategy. The current restrictions on cigarette advertisements, for example, have caused significant changes in the tobacco industry. Cigarette manufacturers have to rethink their entire marketing strategy in view of these changes. Pressure is also exerted on companies to implement affirmative action programmes. Research is required to formulate a response to these changes.

■ *Technological environment*. The rate of change in the technological environment is unprecedented in the history of the world. The popularity of the World Wide Web has spurred demand for digital cameras, particularly for online images. To be competitive, all companies must keep abreast of information about technological changes that may impact their productivity and, in some instances, their ability to survive.

## THE COMPUTER IN DIRECT MARKETING[7]

The computer has been the driving force behind the growing importance of direct marketing by means of extensive databases which enable it to become focused and individual. The decreasing cost of computer technology is making it ever-more affordable to advertisers. The introduction of direct response television (telemarketing), with the advent of toll-free numbers, permits immediate response.

Marketers must therefore develop and implement strategies, and those strategies must constantly be revised as required by changing environments. This means marketers constantly need information – they need information provided by marketing research. Without marketing research information, it is difficult – if not impossible, for management to make sound decisions or to implement the marketing concept properly.

### 3.2.4 Marketing research identifies and defines marketing opportunities and problems

To identify and define marketing opportunities means to define those wants and needs in the market that are not being met by the competition. Opportunities and problems are everywhere, but decision makers need information to help identify and define them adequately. This information is acquired by way of conducting regular research.

> **IDENTIFYING MARKETING OPPORTUNITIES BY MEANS OF RESEARCH**
>
> ■ Many food processing companies such as Campbell's (for example, soup) and Gero (for example, yoghurt) have discovered opportunities arising from consumers' increasing concerns about health, weight and diet and have introduced new foods to the market that are low in cholesterol, fat, sodium and sugar. Campbell's and Gero's research has revealed that there is an opportunity in the market for 'intelligent cuisine'.
>
> ■ People have become more concerned about environmental hazards and the problem with waste in landfills. One company took advantage of this opportunity by developing a 90% recycled paint in cans that are themselves recyclable.

## 3.2.5 Marketing research monitors marketing performance

Monitoring marketing strategies once they are implemented is a way of maintaining control over the success of a new product or service. Any control system requires feedback of information to management. Marketing research brings that information to management personnel, allowing them to compare actual performance with desired performance standards.

## 3.2.6 Marketing research improves our understanding of the marketing process

Some marketing research is conducted to expand our basic knowledge of marketing, known as **basic** research. Typical of such research would be attempts to define and classify certain marketing phenomena and to determine optimum methods for carrying out marketing activities, for example, studies to determine optimum returns on promotional expenditures or studies to determine the operating characteristics of the most profitable firms within an industry.

This type of research is conducted on an ongoing basis by Unisa's Bureau of Market Research.

## BASIC RESEARCH: BUREAU OF MARKET RESEARCH (BMR)

Research conducted by the BMR to extend the body of business knowledge includes:

- Educational levels of the different population groups of South Africa.

- Annual population increases and growth rates of the South African population.

- Expenditure within townships by type of retailer.

- Outlets where township retailers buy their stock.

- Estimated growth of South African youth market by population group.

- Household expenditure by population group.

- Average annual household income by population group.

Basic research thus attempts to expand the frontiers of knowledge; it is research not aimed at a specific pragmatic problem. Basic research hopes to provide further confirmation for an existing theory or to learn more about a concept. For example, basic research might test a hypothesis on high-involvement decision making or consumer information processing. In the long run, basic research helps us to understand more about the world in which we live.

Most marketing research is conducted to improve our understanding of the marketplace, to find out why a strategy failed, or to reduce uncertainty in management decision making. All research conducted for these purposes is called *applied* research. For example, should the price of frozen dinners be raised by 40 cents? What name should Nissan select for the new car? Which advertisement has the highest level of recall: A or B?

Marketing research is not the only source of information available to decision makers. Information is also supplied by the various components of the marketing information system (MIS) of which marketing research is one.

## RESEARCH CAN PRODUCE RESULTS

- A construction company in San Francisco in the United States was trying to gain a competitive edge. Management decided to do marketing research, and asked their customers about the competitors' worst habits. The customers told them about some of these, which included being impolite, uncaring about the dirt they brought into a house, and staff and equipment that looked shoddy. This was not acceptable to the majority of their customers, who were fairly wealthy.

  This information convinced the construction company managers to improve the company's image. They bought new equipment, which they kept spotless, trained their workers to be polite, and dressed them well to project a good image.

  The research and changes paid off. In less than two years, they increased their annual sales by 500%.

## 3.3    THE MARKETING INFORMATION SYSTEM

### 3.3.1    Information management

Data and information are not the same. Information is data that have been converted into a useful form for decision making – for solving a problem.[8] It is relevant, timely, accurate and cost-effective, and it reduces risk in decision making. Marketers face an immense volume of raw data generated internally and externally. If these data are to be useful, the data flow must be managed.

Marketers must consider the cost of collecting and converting data into information when specifying their informational needs. Seldom will they have all the information they want. Thus the cost of additional information must be weighed against its value for planning, implementing and controlling marketing operations.

The company's salesforce should also be trained in intelligence gathering. Its close contact with the market can make it a useful data source for manufacturers, retailers and wholesalers. Too often, however, salespeople are trained only in selling techniques.

Many companies develop a marketing information system (MIS) to gather, sort, analyse, store and distribute relevant and timely marketing information to managers continuously.[9]

The MIS is part of a company's overall information network that integrates electronic records from all the company's functional areas. The purpose of an MIS is to help marketing managers make better decisions. It guides the planning process and leads to meaningful marketing goals and objectives. Having the right information available at the right time also enables managers to make on-the-spot decisions when unforeseen events threaten to derail the marketing plan.

We can now define a marketing information system (MIS) as a system '. . . *for generating and managing a flow of information for marketing decision making*'.[10]

### 3.3.2  Components of a marketing information system

Marketing information systems differ according to the type of company and industry. A small company usually has a simple MIS and a large company has an extensive one. A simple MIS, as illustrated in Figure 3.1, consists of two data components: routine data and special purpose data.

### FIGURE 3.1  A SIMPLE MARKETING INFORMATION SYSTEM

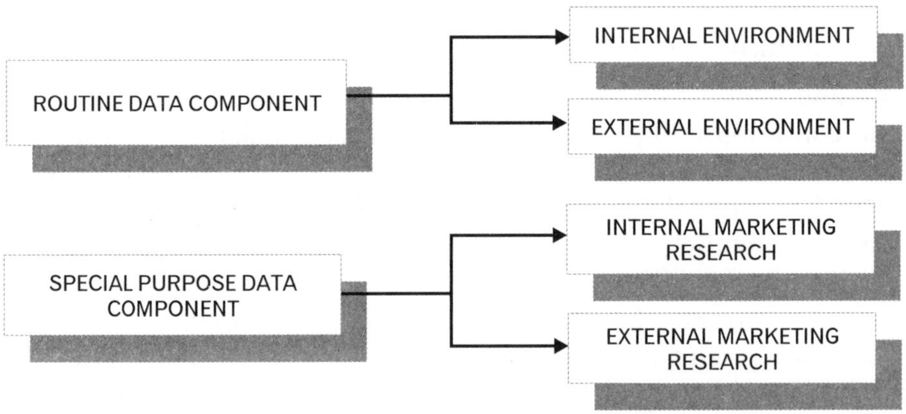

Source: Martins, J.H; Loubser, M and Van Wyk, H de J. 1996. *Marketing research: a South African approach*. Pretoria: University of South Africa Press, p 14.

For a local independent retailer, the routine data component would include, for example, routine information from internal sources such as sales, stocks, debtors and creditors. From external sources information such as local population growth, competitive activities and trade association statistics can be collected on a regular basis. The special purpose component includes marketing research, for example where a retailer engages a marketing research organisation to determine the

© Juta

feasibility of a particular retail space in a new shopping centre (external marketing research). The retailer conducting certain research projects on his/her own, for example, a survey among existing customers to determine their degree of satisfaction with its services, constitutes internal marketing research (launched from internal sources).

Larger companies which have the necessary resources usually operate an extensive marketing information system. The major components of an extensive marketing information system and the interaction among its components are indicated in Figure 3.2.

## FIGURE 3.2 AN EXTENSIVE MARKETING INFORMATION SYSTEM

| INTERNAL REPORTING SUBSYSTEM | MARKETING INTELIGENCE SUBSYSTEM |
|---|---|
| ACCOUNTING REPORTS<br>PRODUCTION REPORTS<br>SALES REPORTS<br>QUALITY CONTROL REPORTS<br>ENGINEERING REPORTS<br>GOODS RETURNED REPORTS | CONSUMERS<br>COMPETITORS<br>SUPPLIERS<br>PROFESSIONAL ASSOCIATIONS<br>GOVERNMENT BODIES |
| STATISTICAL SUBSYSTEM | INTERNAL AND/OR EXTERNAL MARKETING RESEARCH SUBSYSTEM |
| STATISTICAL MODELS<br>FORECASTING TECHNIQUES<br>DYNAMIC MODELING<br>GAME THEORY | PROBLEM DEFINITION<br>RESEARCH DESIGN<br>DATA COLLECTION AND PROCESSING<br>DATA ANALYSIS<br>REPORTING |

Source: Marx, S. and Van der Walt, A. 1993. *Marketing management*. Cape Town: Juta, p 139.

The four major components of an extensive marketing information system, as indicated in Figure 3.2 are:

1. An internal reporting subsystem.

2. A marketing intelligence subsystem.

3. A statistical subsystem.

4. A marketing research system.

These four components will now be discussed in more detail.

### 3.3.2.1 The internal reporting subsystem

Various reports are prepared internally by companies. These reports contain information about the historical performance results of the company. By way of this information, important opportunities and threats can be timeously identified. Important reports emanate from, among others, the accounting department, the production department, the sales department and the quality control department. These reports include accounting reports, production reports, sales reports, engineering reports and goods returned reports.[11]

---

**SALESPEOPLE RECORD ORDERS**

Salespeople, for example, record orders on their laptop computers and this information is sent via modem to the company headquarters, which notifies the warehouse to expedite delivery. The information recorded during this process – customer name, location, goods ordered, prices, delivery location, method of delivery, date, and so on – becomes the information ingredients in the internal reports system. The internal reporting subsystem ensures that information generated is recorded, stored and made available for retrieval by managers.

---

We referred to Sears, the successful American retailer, earlier. Let us look how Sears uses internal records in making marketing decisions.[12]

---

**USING INTERNAL RECORDS IN MAKING MARKETING DECISIONS**

Sears uses internal records as a marketing tool. Marketing managers use computerised information on Sears' 40 million customers to promote special product and service offers to such diverse target segments as gardening service providers, appliance buyers and expectant mothers. For example, Sears keeps track of the appliance purchases of each customer and promotes special service-package deals to customers who have bought several appliances but have not purchased maintenance contracts for them. South African retailers are also increasingly using available data about consumers to their advantage.

---

### 3.3.2.2 The marketing intelligence subsystem

This subsystem consists of procedures and sources whereby management obtain information concerning current and relevant occurrences in the marketing environment.

Whereas an internal reporting system focuses on *results*, the intelligence system focuses on *happenings* in the marketing environment. The marketing intelligence subsystem includes both informal and formal information-gathering procedures. *Informal information-gathering* procedures involve such activities as scanning newspapers, magazines and trade publications. *Formal information-gathering* activities may be conducted by staff members who are assigned the specific task of looking for anything that seems pertinent to the company or industry. They then edit and disseminate this information to the appropriate members of the company.

---

**PURCHASING INFORMATION**

Some companies find it advantageous to purchase information from speciality organisations on a regular basis. In South Africa, International Business Information Systems (IBIS), which has an association with the internationally reputable AC Nielsen company, is well known for the retail audits which it regularly conducts. This information includes aspects such as market shares, retail prices, inventory levels and marketing communications.

---

### 3.3.2.3 Statistical subsystem

The statistical subsystem is a composition of a statistical database and the application of advanced statistical procedures and techniques. The purpose of this system is to create projections, scenarios and models which provide a better grasp of the alternatives for decision making. Decision making always takes place in conditions of risk and uncertainty. With this subsystem, an attempt is made to quantify the probable results of various possible actions of marketing management.

A variety of statistical data series is stored and regularly updated in the statistical subsystem. These serve as bases for the application of statistical techniques (with multiple variables), forecasting techniques and the creation of models. These models allow companies to ask 'what if' questions.

Answers to these questions are then immediately available for decision making. A model can, for example, illustrate the probable effect of a change in consumer price on consumer behaviour.

### 3.3.2.4 Marketing research subsystem

The marketing research subsystem gathers information not gathered by the other MIS component subsystems. Marketing research studies are conducted for a *specific situation* facing the company. It is unlikely that other components of MIS have generated the *particular* information needed for the *specific* situation. This is why people in the industry sometimes refer to marketing research studies as '*ad hoc*' studies. *Ad hoc* is a Latin term meaning 'with respect to a specific purpose'. Marketing research projects, unlike the other components of the MIS, are not continuous – they have a beginning and an end. This is why marketing research studies are sometimes referred to as 'projects'.

---

### MARKETING RESEARCH PROBLEMS

- A company that suspects a change in consumer preferences would investigate this problem by means of a marketing research project.

- A bank may wish to measure its competitiveness. Marketing research is then conducted.

- A company may want to develop target customer profiles. Marketing research is then employed.

- An advertising agency may need to know more about the scheduling of advertisements and can use marketing research to solve this problem.

- A manufacturer of cosmetics may need to know which packaging would be the most acceptable and conducts marketing research among customers to accomplish this.

---

### 3.3.3 The interaction between the components of a marketing information system

Figure 3.3 illustrates the dynamic interaction between the four subsystems of the marketing information system of a soft drinks manufacturer.

In Figure 3.3, we can see that the internal reporting subsystem revealed that in KwaZulu-Natal there had been a 50% decrease in soft drink sales for December. More information about this phenomenon was gained via marketing intelligence. Retailers mentioned that there had been a price reduction by the main competitor in KwaZulu-Natal. The next step was to use the statistical subsystem to develop a model of the behaviour patterns of KwaZulu-Natal consumers. However, no information about consumer preferences was available. A marketing research project was then launched to determine consumer demand for soft drinks in KwaZulu-Natal. Market Research Africa was instructed to investigate the problem and to provide information. On the basis of these research results, marketing management would be in a position to make appropriate decisions which included either changing the packaging or maintaining the price level if it was discovered that the consumers were not concerned with the prices.

FIGURE 3.3    INTERACTION OF THE COMPONENTS OF A
             MARKETING INFORMATION SYSTEM OF A
             SOFT DRINKS MANUFACTURER

| COMPONENT | INFORMATION | DECISION MAKING |
|---|---|---|
| Internal reporting subsystem | Sales reports for KwaZulu-Natal indicate a 50% decrease in sales for December. | Ascertain the causes by way of the marketing intelligence subsystem. |
| Marketing intelligence subsystem | Retailers mention a price reduction by the main competitor in KwaZulu-Natal. | Use the statistical subsystem to determine the probable effects of various alternative decisions. |
| Statistical subsystem | Develop a model of the behaviour patterns of KwaZulu-Natal consumers concerning soft drinks purchasing. *Problem: Information about consumer preferences is not available.* | Launch a marketing research project to determine the factors in KwaZulu-Natal consumer demand for soft drinks, as well as their relative importance. |

Figure 3.3 is continued on page 90.

| COMPONENT | INFORMATION | DECISION MAKING |
|---|---|---|
| Marketing research subsystem | Give instruction to Market Research Africa to investigate and provide information. | Marketing management makes appropriate decisions, for example:<br><br>■ Change packaging because competitors' packaging is better.<br><br>■ Monitor sales on a weekly basis.<br><br>■ Launch a marketing communications campaign to strengthen brand loyalty among consumers.<br><br>■ Maintain price levels because consumers are not price sensitive. |

Source: Marx, S and Van der Walt, A. 1993. *Marketing management.* Cape Town: Juta, p 142

We will now focus on one component of the marketing information system, namely marketing research.

## 3.4  MARKETING RESEARCH

Some of marketing management's most important decisions rely on information gathered by research that specifically addresses the decision maker's concerns. For example:

### MANY DECISIONS REQUIRE INFORMATION

■ Sales personnel rely on research to provide them with feedback on sales performance or to identify likely purchasers.

■ Media planners need information to determine which specific magazines or television shows will most likely be seen by a market segment.

■ Advertising executives need feedback to 'flesh out' the needs and wants of target consumers.

■ Brand managers need to determine how their product is perceived in the marketplace, especially relative to other competing brands.

Some marketers conduct limited, low-cost research projects by searching the MIS database and gathering the required information. More typically, the marketer has a problem that requires very specific information and must rely on marketing research to gather data systematically.

Large companies like Coca-Cola have extensive marketing research capabilities to conduct their own research. Depending on the information required and the complexity of the research problem, companies may hire research companies to conduct all or part of their research.

---

**FINDING MARKETING RESEARCH COMPANIES ON THE INTERNET**

The Internet is a powerful tool for identifying research companies that provide particular types of services and for conducting a preliminary review of these companies. Most research companies' sites are e-mail-enabled. Therefore, after research buyers have identified likely candidates through preliminary research and evaluation, they can send e-mail to these organisations, requesting additional information. A few companies even have RFP (Requests For Proposal) forms on their sites which permit the research buyer to submit an RFP via e-mail. In this way, one can review the services offered by marketing research companies.

---

## 3.4.1  Steps in the marketing research process

The marketing research process is a series of carefully thought-out steps designed to attain a specific objective. In this section we will look at the different steps in the marketing research process.

There are various reasons why marketing research is undertaken. Consider the following:

---

**REASONS WHY MARKETING RESEARCH NEEDS TO BE CONDUCTED**

- Top management instructs marketing management to investigate the possibility of an attractive marketing opportunity.

- Marketing management must develop a marketing strategy for a new product.

---

■ There is a sustained decline in sales of one of the company's products and marketing management is instructed to determine the cause and recommend remedial action.

As we can see, each of these reasons is in some way unique, and the procedures followed in the research process of each will vary to some extent. For example, the research process in the case of an investigation into a decline in sales will differ from an investigation into the development of a marketing strategy for a new product.

Although the research processes or procedures may differ for different types of problems or opportunities, a marketing research investigation consists of two parts: a **preliminary** marketing investigation and a **formal** marketing investigation. Both investigations may need to be conducted, but if the problem is solved during the preliminary investigation, a formal investigation will not be required. However, the formal investigation cannot be conducted satisfactorily unless a preliminary investigation has been done.

## FIGURE 3.4 STEPS IN THE MARKETING RESEARCH PROCESS

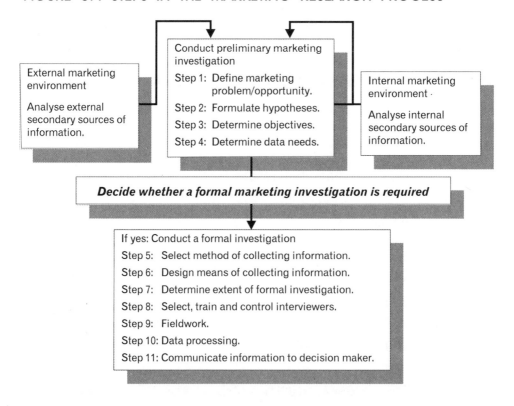

External marketing environment

Analyse external secondary sources of information.

Conduct preliminary marketing investigation

Step 1: Define marketing problem/opportunity.

Step 2: Formulate hypotheses.

Step 3: Determine objectives.

Step 4: Determine data needs.

Internal marketing environment

Analyse internal secondary sources of information.

*Decide whether a formal marketing investigation is required*

If yes: Conduct a formal investigation

Step 5: Select method of collecting information.

Step 6: Design means of collecting information.

Step 7: Determine extent of formal investigation.

Step 8: Select, train and control interviewers.

Step 9: Fieldwork.

Step 10: Data processing.

Step 11: Communicate information to decision maker.

The marketing research process may be viewed as a number of consecutive steps undertaken to obtain the required marketing information. Although authors differ on the number of stages involved in the research process, they all agree that some basic stages should be included. Figure 3.4 reflects a logical 11-step approach to the marketing research process which will be discussed in detail.

### 3.4.1.1 The preliminary marketing investigation

### Step 1: Identify and define the problem or opportunity

This first step of the marketing research process entails a clear definition of the nature and extent of the problem or opportunity. Often there is only a vague feeling that 'something is wrong' and management has at its disposal contradictory pieces of information, reports, opinions and symptoms such as a decline in sales figures. In order to take appropriate action, it is essential to know more about the problem or opportunity. Thus, the real nature and extent of the problem should be determined. For example, if a decline in sales of a company's products has been discovered, further investigation (by means of small-scale research), may reveal that the decline is restricted to the KwaZulu-Natal area.

Typical problems (or opportunities) that may require a marketing research investigation are the following:

**PROBLEMS (OR OPPORTUNITIES) THAT MUST BE INVESTIGATED**

- Which of two package designs best conveys the desired image for the product?
- More general information for a planning decision is required.
- A brand manager planning packaging changes may want to know what features of a package on a grocery shelf create interest in consumers.
- As changes occur in the company's external environment, a marketing manager is faced with the questions, 'Should we change the existing marketing strategy and, if so, how?'
- Marketing research may be needed to evaluate product, promotion, distribution, or pricing alternatives.
- Marketing research may be needed to establish and evaluate new market opportunities.

Once a problem has been identified, the marketing researcher is approached. The first responsibility of the researcher, whether from internal staff or an outside consulting company, is to work with the marketing manager to define precisely the problem[13]. Proper definition of a problem also provides guidance and direction for the entire process.

In an attempt to define the exact nature of the problem or opportunity and to gain a better understanding of the environment within which the problem has occurred, it may be necessary to conduct small-scale research.

## SMALL-SCALE RESEARCH AT TOYOTA

About ten years ago, Toyota launched its minibus, the Venture, which has proved to be one of the most successful new motorcar products in decades. Toyota needs to understand the changing needs and wishes of the target market to maintain its market share. The problem in this case is that Toyota must deliver exceptional value to the target customer to maintain and build market share and profits.

In order to identify and define the problem, Toyota researchers, in conducting small-scale research, may act as follows:

■ Review several existing studies and articles on driving trends.

■ Competing dealers could be visited to determine which features they are promoting and their selling techniques.

■ A small-scale survey of consumers might be developed along with interviews of company executives.

■ Small groups of consumers may be consulted to discuss driving habits.

■ Experts could be consulted. For example, the researcher could seek out publishers of car magazines and researchers at the Department of Transport.

The marketing researcher now possesses information on the nature and extent of the problem or opportunity. The next step is to formulate hypotheses that need to be investigated.

## Step 2: Formulate hypotheses

In this step, specific factors which can be identified as influencing factors or the causes of the problem or opportunity are identified. From this group of factors, some are selected which are considered important enough to be further investigated, and these are called **hypotheses**. Hypotheses can thus be seen as tentative solutions or actions for the problem or opportunity.

For example, let us assume that a company experiences a decline in sales. There are many factors or variables which may be the cause of this decline in sales.

### POSSIBLE CAUSES OF DECLINE IN SALES

- Certain actions by competitors – for example, price discounting.

- A change in consumer preferences.

- The employment of an inefficient product, distribution, promotion or price strategy.

- A combination of all these variables.

One or more of these possible causes may be identified as the possible cause(s) of the decline in sales, in other words, one of these statements may be termed the **hypothesis**.

If all these possible causes need to be investigated, several research projects would have to be undertaken. Further investigation, however, may reveal that only one of the possible causes should be investigated, for example, a change in consumer preferences. This will then be translated into a hypothesis for further investigation.

Confirming or rejecting the hypotheses is a crucial phase of the research project. During this process, new information may come to light and it may be deemed necessary to redefine certain problems (or hypotheses). The following example illustrates how a problem can be redefined:[14]

### REDEFINITION OF A PROBLEM

The sales manager of a local potato crisp manufacturer notices that sales are declining and interprets the problem as ineffective advertising (hypothesis).

The researcher is therefore asked to investigate the effectiveness of the company's advertising. In talking to salespeople, wholesalers and retailers of the company's products, however, the researcher discovers that the support for the product began to decline when a rival company introduced a new product that gave them a larger margin on sales. Retailers are therefore making more profit by selling the rival's product.

This gives the researcher a new perspective on the problem. An investigation of advertising effectiveness will not help solve the problem. This hypothesis must then be rejected and redefined as 'competitive pricing and profit margin tactics'.

### Step 3: Determining the research objectives

Once the problem has been identified and clearly defined, and hypotheses have been formulated, the researcher can determine the objectives of the research project. These objectives are stated in terms of the precise information necessary and desired to solve the marketing problem. The objectives must relate directly to the hypotheses formulated during step two. In fact, the hypotheses become the research objectives. For example:

### RESEARCH OBJECTIVES

A decline in sales in one of the company's products has been established (in other words, the symptom). The problem has been identified and defined and subsequently one hypothesis has been formulated, namely that 'consumer preferences have changed'. The research objective in this case could be 'to investigate consumer preferences'.

Well-formulated objectives serve as a road map in developing the research project. They also serve as a standard which enables managers to evaluate the quality and value of the work.

Were the objectives met and do the recommendations flow logically from the objectives and the research findings? Objectives must be as specific and unambiguous as possible. Putting the objectives in writing avoids the problem of wondering whether the information that has been received is, in fact, what is required[15].

In general, a research investigation will have one of four basic objectives:

1. To explore.

2. To describe.

3. To test hypotheses (causal research).

4. To predict.

These four objectives will now be described in more detail.

■ **To explore**. The primary objective of exploratory research is to provide insights into, and an understanding of, the problem confronting the researcher (as explained earlier). Once the problem has been clearly defined, exploratory research can be useful in identifying alternative courses of action. Researchers conduct exploratory research when they need more information about the problem, when tentative hypotheses need to be formulated more specifically, or when new hypotheses are required.[16] Because exploratory research is aimed at gaining additional information about a topic and generating possible hypotheses to test, it is described as informal research.

## EXAMPLES OF EXPLORATORY RESEARCH

■ Visiting the library to read published secondary data.

■ Asking customers and salespeople their opinions about a company, its products, services and prices.

■ Simply observing everyday company practices.

The researcher investigates whatever sources he/she desires, to the extent that he/she feels is necessary in order to gain a good understanding of the problem.

■ **To describe**. Descriptive research is necessary when knowledge about a particular market or marketing aspect is vague. It includes research designed to provide answers to questions regarding the who, what, when, where and how of a topic.

For example, an enterprise that is considering entering the hospitality industry may have identified the 'conference market' as one of their target markets. This market, however, needs further clarification and must be described more clearly. Descriptive research may also be necessary where the nature of the competition in a particular industry is vague. Soft drink marketers also use this type of research to describe the characteristics and wants of different groups of consumers.

■ *To test hypotheses (causal research)*. If the objective is to test hypotheses about the relationship between an independent and a dependent variable, the researcher engages in causal research. Causal research would be used in the following example:

### INDEPENDENT AND DEPENDENT VARIABLES IN CAUSAL RESEARCH

■ What would happen to sales if prices are reduced? Price is the independent variable, that is, the factor being manipulated. The sales level is the dependent variable that will be affected when the independent variable (price) is changed (price is reduced).

■ What would happen to customer awareness of the product if advertising were to be increased? Advertising is the independent variable, while awareness is the dependent variable that will be affected when the independent variable (advertising) is changed (advertising increased).

Causal research is therefore used to obtain evidence of cause-and-effect relationships. It attempts to determine the extent to which changes in the one variable cause changes in another variable.

### CAUSAL RESEARCH VERSUS DESCRIPTIVE RESEARCH

Descriptive research may suggest that a price reduction is associated with increased sales of a product, but it does not definitely suggest that a decrease in price was the actual *cause* of the sales increase. Sales may have increased because of other factors, such as an increase in customer buying power or a decline in competitors' marketing efforts.

Causal research, on the other hand, tries to show either that the price cut (independent variable) is the cause of increased sales (dependent variable) or that the price cut is *not* the cause of increased sales. This requires that the researcher keep all factors other than price and sales constant – at best, a difficult task.

■ ***Predictive research.*** Predictive research is conducted to forecast future values, for example, sales income, market shares and retail orders. Political pollsters use predictive research to forecast how many people will vote for a particular candidate in an upcoming election. Businesses engage in sales forecasting to predict sales of the products during a specific time period, for example, a financial year.

### Step 4:   Determine the data needs

In this step, the research objectives must be translated into specific data needs. This means that it must be determined what information is required and from which sources this information can be obtained in order to test the hypotheses so that the problem can be solved. For example:

### SPECIFIC DATA NEEDS: THE SOUTH AFRICAN POLICE SERVICE (SAPS)

Suppose the SAPS wants to establish what steps it can take to improve the quality of recruits. The information necessary to satisfy this research objective might include:

■ A detailed description of recruiting incentives currently being offered by the SAPS.

■ Young people's attitudes toward existing recruiting incentives offered by the SAPS.

■ The demographic and lifestyle characteristics of current police enlistees who are high achievers.

■ A detailed description of recruiting activities currently in use at recruiting centres.

■ A forecast of unemployment rates for the next decade.

In determining the type of data needed, the problem (step 1), the hypotheses (step 2) and the objectives (step 3) must be considered. Specific data will be needed in order to confirm or reject each hypothesis that has been formulated.

Researchers distinguish between secondary and primary data. **Secondary data** are data that were previously collected by people either inside or outside the company to meet their needs. If these data can assist in solving the problem, that is, in confirming or rejecting the hypothesis, there may be no reason to collect primary data. Secondary data are usually cheaper and faster to collect, but researchers must always consider their relevance, accuracy, credibility and timeliness.

**Primary data** are data that are collected through original research for a specific purpose. The data must not have been collected previously. The big advantage of primary data is that they relate specifically to the problem at hand. The main disadvantages of primary data are the cost and time required to collect them. Primary data will normally be collected during the next phase of the research process, the formal investigation.

As emphasised above, secondary data should be sought and researched during the preliminary investigation and all efforts should be made to solve the problem at this stage.

Secondary data can come from internal or external sources. The major internal source is company records. Public libraries, trade associations and government publications are important external sources. Population data, for example, may be obtained from detailed census publications. The Bureau of Market Research at Unisa could, for example, be approached on data such as the 'Average annual household income by population group', 'Annual population increases and growth rates of the South African population', and 'Educational levels by population group'.

**Primary data** can also come from internal or external sources. The major internal source is company personnel. Retailers, wholesalers, customers and competitors are important external sources.

The different sources of primary and secondary data are indicated in Figure 3.5 .

Secondary data collected must clearly relate to the hypotheses formulated earlier.

## FIGURE 3.5 SOURCES OF SECONDARY AND PRIMARY DATA

| PRIMARY DATA | | SECONDARY DATA | |
|---|---|---|---|
| Internal sources | External sources | Internal sources | External sources |
| Employees | Consumers<br>Clients<br>Retailers<br>Wholesalers<br>Competitors | Company records | Libraries<br>Industry associations<br>Chambers of industry and commerce<br>Government bodies<br>Marketing research organisations<br>Universities |

Source: Van der Walt, A; Strydom, JW; Marx, S and Jooste CJ. 1996. *Marketing management*. Cape Town: Juta, p 151

### SECONDARY DATA ON THE INTERNET

In the last few years, the rapid development of the Internet and World Wide Web has promised the elimination of much of the drudgery associated with the collection of secondary data.

The Internet allows computers (and the people who use them) to access data, pictures, sound and files throughout the world without regard to their physical location or the type of computer on which the data can be found. The World Wide Web (also called the Web or www) is one component of the Internet which was designed to make transmission of text and images as easy as possible.

If you know the address of a particular Website that contains the secondary data that you are searching for, you can easily access that address by following the correct procedure. Sometimes, however, it can require some hard work and trial and error to find data on the Web. However, as long as you have an Internet connection, you have access to a multitude of sources of information.

If the secondary information obtained can provide enough clarification about the hypothesis, the hypothesis can be confirmed or rejected during the preliminary investigation. The problem may therefore be solved at this stage and it may be resolved not to proceed to a formal marketing investigation. However, if it is felt that the problem has not been solved, or if further information is clearly required, the formal investigation must be conducted. In the following example, the data required and possible sources of data are indicated to test certain hypotheses:

### SECONDARY DATA NEEDED TO TEST HYPOTHESES

| Hypotheses | Data required | Possible sources of data |
|---|---|---|
| (a) The decline in general sales is the result of a drop in the demand for one particular camera. | Analysis of the sales figures of various models of cameras and sales trends. | Sales statistics of the marketing department, discussions with a few dealers. |
| (b) The decline is caused by a drop in sales in a particular area due to a particular sales-person's poor performance. | Data on camera sales in particular sales regions, performance of individual salespeople in these areas. | Statistics of sales/ marketing department on camera sales in different economic regions, and of individual sales-people. |
| (c) The decline is caused by a shift in consumer preferences from photographic to digital cameras. | Data on general camera sales compared with digital cameras and possible reasons for the shift. | Statistics on sales of of the two kinds of cameras, from Department of Customs and Excise or trade associations of camera manufacturers and/or dealers. |

### 3.4.1.2 The formal marketing investigation

### Step 5: Select the method of collecting the information

The researcher can gather primary data through observation, experimentation, focus groups and surveys, as reflected in Figure 3.6. These methods will be discussed in more detail.

## FIGURE 3.6 TYPES AND SOURCES OF DATA AND COLLECTION METHODS

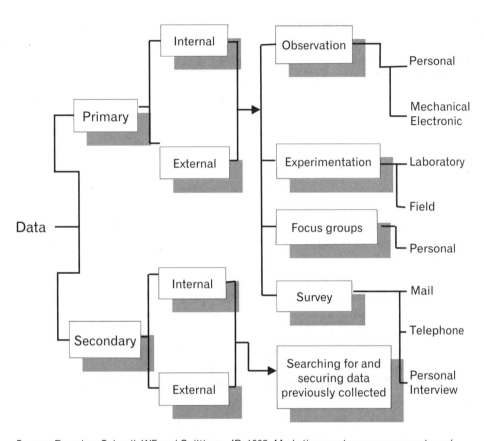

Source: Based on Schoell, WF and Guiltinan, JP. 1995. *Marketing: contemporary concepts and practices*. 6th edition. Englewood Cliffs, NJ: Prentice Hall, p 113.

- **Observation method**. The observation method involves recording the behavioural patterns of people, objects and events in a systematic manner to obtain information about the phenomenon of interest.[17] The observer does not question or communicate with the people being observed. Information may be recorded as the events occur or from records of past events. The disadvantages of this method are the cost of waiting for the phenomenon to occur and the difficulty of measuring the phenomenon in a natural setting. For example, a manufacturer of breakfast cereals who wants to study the attention-producing value of a new package might station observers with cameras and tape recorders in the supermarket aisles where the cereal is displayed. The observers would monitor the actions of shoppers directly.

Other examples of observational research are as follows:

## OBSERVATIONAL RESEARCH[18]

- A museum director wanted to know which of the many exhibits was most popular. A survey did not help. Visitors seemed to want to please the interviewer, and usually said that all the exhibits were interesting. Putting observers near exhibits to record how long visitors spent at each one did not help either, since the curious visitors stood around to see what was being recorded, therefore distorting the value of the exercise. Finally, the museum floors were waxed to a glossy shine. Several weeks later, the floors around the exhibits were inspected. It was easy to tell which exhibits were most popular, based on how much shine had worn off the floor.

- A shopping centre developer wondered if one of his shopping centres was attracting customers from all surrounding areas. He hired a company to record the registration numbers of cars in the parking lot. By using the registration information, the addresses of all shoppers were then obtained and plotted on a map. Very few customers from one particular area were visiting the centre. The developer than aimed direct mail advertising at that area and generated a great deal of new business.

Observation may be more objective than surveys because no questions are asked. The observation method focuses on what people do (direct observation) or on what they did (indirect observation), not on what they say they do or did. Observers, however, can interpret only the behaviour they witness directly. This interpretation may be inaccurate or biased. A shopper may pick up a package of cereal, examine it, and walk away without buying it. The shopper may have wanted to purchase the cereal but may not have had enough money to buy it. An observer, however, might interpret this behaviour as lack of interest in the product. In other words, we do not know why the shopper left the package. Some things such as motives simply cannot be observed.

Artificial observation is often used and is done by way of mechanical or electronic equipment such as the use of the AMPS Peoplemeter II to monitor viewing patterns of selected households in South Africa.[19]

■ **Experimentation**. Experimentation research involves testing something in controlled conditions. Conclusions are then drawn about the wider environment. This involves the gathering of primary data by manipulating an independent variable (such as advertising or price) to observe the effect of the change on a dependent variable (such as sales).[20] By attempting to hold all other factors constant while manipulating price, it might be possible to estimate how many units of a product would be demanded at various prices. Researchers often conduct experimentation in a field setting. The field setting is realistic but is difficult to control, and it is almost impossible to ensure that test conditions will be the same as conditions in the real market.

## EXPERIMENTATION IN A FIELD SETTING

An advertising manager wants to test the effectiveness of a proposed newspaper advertisement and selects two cities similar in population characteristics, income distribution and so on. One is the control city and the other the test city. The advertisement appears in the test city's newspaper but not in the control city's newspaper. After the advertisement appears, sales of the product are recorded. Any difference in sales in the two cities is attributed to the advertisement.

Three assumptions in the above situation are made. Firstly, two or more similar cities can be found. Secondly, the control city's environment can be controlled. Thirdly, test conditions are the same as those that will exist when the advertisement is run in the real market. However, locating two almost identical cities for testing is not always easy. Also, if a rival withdraws its product in the control city, sales of the researcher's product might increase. If test city sales are lower than those in the control city, the researcher might incorrectly conclude that the advertisement is ineffective. Thus it is almost impossible to ensure that test conditions will be the same as conditions in the real market.

Let us also look at how experimental research helped to solve the following problem:[21]

## MARS CHOCOLATE BARS: A SWEET SUCCESS

Mars chocolate bar company was losing customers to other sweet and snack companies and wanted to identify the reason. Surveys showed that many customers thought that the Mars bar, which was not being sold in a larger size, was too small. They also did not want to pay more for a larger bar. Mars' marketing manager wanted to know if making their chocolate bar bigger would increase sales to offset the higher cost. To decide, they needed more information.

The company carefully varied the size of Mars bars sold in different markets. Otherwise, the marketing mix stayed the same. Researchers then tracked sales in each market to determine the effect of the different sizes. They saw a significant difference immediately. It was clear that the added sales would more than offset the cost of a bigger Mars bar. Marketing managers at Mars therefore made a decision that took them in the opposite direction (of bigger chocolate bars) to other sweet companies.

■ *Focus groups*. A focus group is a small group of people, usually between 8 and 12, brought together and guided by a moderator through an unstructured, spontaneous discussion about some topic.[22] It is called a 'focus' group because the moderator serves to focus the discussion on the topic and does not let the group move off on tangents or irrelevant points. The goal of a focus group is to draw out ideas, feelings and experiences about a certain issue that would be obscured or stifled by more structured methods of data collection. The use of a small group allows the operation of group dynamics and aids in making the participants feel comfortable in a strange environment.

Focus groups have been useful in understanding basic shifts in consumer lifestyles, values and purchase patterns. Usually the focus group members share homogeneous characteristics such as similarities in age (they may all be in their early 30s), job situations (they may all be sales managers), family composition (they may all have preschool children), or even leisure pursuits (they may all play tennis). For example, a mother's club focus group's opinions are canvassed to determine their desires, preferences and buying behaviour of various brands of cheese.

By conducting a group that is as homogeneous as possible with respect to demographic and other characteristics, the researcher is assured that differences in these variables will be less likely to confuse the issue being discussed. The focus group can furnish qualitative data on such things as consumer language, emotional and behavioural reaction to advertising; lifestyle; relationships; the product category and specific brand; and unconscious consumer motivations relative to product design, packaging, promotion or any other facet of the marketing programme being studied. It must, however, be remembered that focus group results are qualitative and not perfectly representative of the general population, thus limiting the reliability of this type of data collection.

## CYBER FOCUS GROUPS

The newest development in group interviews is the online or cyber focus group. A number of organisations are currently offering this new means of conducting focus groups on the Internet.

The research firm builds a database of respondents via a screening questionnaire on its Website. When a client approaches them with a need for a particular focus group, they access their database and identify individuals who appear to qualify. E-mail is sent to these individuals, asking them to log on to a particular site at a particular time scheduled for the group. A moderator runs the group by typing in questions online for all to see. The group operates in a chat-room-type environment so that all participants see all questions and responses. The complete text of the focus group is captured and is available for review after the group session.

- **Survey method.** Survey research is the gathering of primary data from respondents by mail, by telephone, or in person. Survey research can be highly structured or unstructured. In a structured survey, all respondents are asked the same list of questions in the same way. In an unstructured survey interviewers are free to ask their own questions to encourage respondents to reply as they wish. Three types of data are usually sought in survey research: *facts*, *opinions*, and *motives*. These types of data are explained in the box below.

## TYPES OF DATA IN SURVEY RESEARCH

- In a *factual survey*, respondents are asked questions such as 'What type of car do you drive?'

- In an *opinion survey*, respondents are asked to give opinions, although they believe they are reporting facts, for example, an opinion survey question is 'What type of toothpaste tastes better?'

- In a *motivational survey*, respondents are asked to interpret and report their motives. These surveys ask 'why' questions such as 'Why do you holiday in Cape Town every year?'

### Step 6: Design the form of collecting the information

The next step is to design a form or instrument whereby the information is to be collected. *Mechanical and electronic devices* and *questionnaires* are two types of research instruments used for the collection of primary data.

- *Mechanical and electronic equipment.* Mechanical and electronic equipment are instruments such as galvanometers, tachistoscopes, cameras and electronic and mechanical meters. These instruments range from simple counting meters (for example the number of people passing through a turnstile) to sophisticated reaction-measurement instruments (for example, emotional reaction to a specific advertisement). Some researchers use personal computers to conduct interviews. Many researchers believe that respondents will provide more private information to a computer than they will in a face-to-face interview.

- *Questionnaires*. The most common method for gathering primary data is the questionnaire. In designing a questionnaire, researchers must exercise great care in deciding which questions to ask, the content and phrasing of questions, how to word the questions, how to sequence the questions, and the format of the questions.

The first important aspect of the questionnaire is *question content and phrasing*.[23] It is important to keep the wording of the questions simple, clear and concise, to fit in with the vocabulary level of the respondents.

In surveys conducted among the South African population, for example, the questions should be worded in such a way that even the less sophisticated and less educated understand the questions. Therefore, it is important to have a clear idea of the target population.

In designing the **wording** of a question, leading questions should be avoided which may suggest or imply certain answers as this could be construed as a cue in the question to what the answer should be. Often the question can reflect the researcher's viewpoint. A biasing question includes words or phrases that are emotionally coloured and that suggest approval or disapproval, for example, 'Do you agree or disagree with the South African Dental Association's position that advertising presweetened cereal to children is . . .?' The mere suggestion that an attitude is associated with a prestigious organisation can seriously bias the respondent's reply.

Another important aspect is the **sequence of questions**.[24] The sequence of questions can influence the nature of the respondents' answers and can cause serious errors in the survey findings. It is advisable to use the funnel approach by moving from the general to the particular, since a change of subject may disturb the logical flow of the interview unless there are links between subjects.

The first questions should therefore be simple and should attempt to generate interest, their main intention being to put the respondents at ease and motivate them to react to the succeeding questions without suspicion. Sensitive questions (for example, income, qualifications and age of respondent) should be positioned as near to the end of the questionnaire as possible.

The **question format,** that is, the form in which the questions are presented, is also very important. **Open-ended questions** such as those in Figure 3.8(a) do not provide respondents with a choice of answers; instead, respondents formulate their own answers in their own words.[25] **Closed questions** (see Figure 3.8(b)) give respondents all the possible answers to each question; respondents then simply choose one. Ambiguous questions and leading questions should be avoided, while personal questions, for example, the respondent's age, should be placed at the end of the questionnaire (see Figure 3.8(c)).

Figure 3.7 shows a hypothetical questionnaire with commentary about the quality of the questions.

## FIGURE 3.7 EXAMPLES OF OPEN-ENDED QUESTIONS, CLOSED QUESTIONS AND FAULTY QUESTIONS

| QUESTION FORM (a) | QUESTION FORM (b) | QUESTION FORM (c) |
|---|---|---|
| **1. Totally Open**<br>'What do you think of Ford South Africa?'<br>_____<br>_____<br>**2. Sentence Completion**<br>'In buying a new car, the most important thing to keep in mind is<br>_____ '<br>**3. Word Association**<br>'Domestic cars' _____<br>'Foreign cars' _____<br>'Auto dealerships' ___<br>'Ford' _____<br>**4. Picture Completion** | **1. Dichotomous**<br>'Do you think air bags should be required equipment on all new cars?'<br>Yes ☐<br>No ☐<br>**2. Multiple Choice**<br>'What age group are you in?'<br>20 or under<br>21 to 29 ___<br>30 to 39 ___<br>40 to 49 ___<br>50 to 59 ___<br>60 or over ___<br>**3. Semantic Differential**<br>'Ford of South Africa'<br>Large _ _ _ _ Small<br>Modern _ _ _ Old-fashioned<br>**4. Rating Scale**<br>'Customer service at Ford dealers is :'<br>1 ___ Excellent<br>2 ___ Very good<br>3 ___ Good<br>4 ___ Fair<br>5 ___ Poor | **1 What is your age?**<br>Too personal a question to begin a questionnaire. Should be at the end and provide age ranges.<br>**2 What kind of car(s) do you presently own?**<br>Ambiguous question. What does 'kind' mean? Brand name, size, model, country of origin, convertible or hard top? What if the respondent leases instead of owns?<br>**3 How much did you pay for security equipment the last time you bought a new car?**<br>The respondent will probably be unable to provide this information.<br>**4 Don't you think passive restraint systems make for safer and more economical cars than other types of systems?**<br>Yes ☐     No ☐<br>What does passive restraint mean? Two subjects are being discussed - safety and economy. It is also a leading question.<br>**5 Have you ever felt guilty for driving your car after you had too much to drink, thereby inviting a serious accident?**<br>Yes ☐     No ☐<br>Most people would probably not be willing to answer this question. |

Source: Adapted from Schoell, WF and Guiltinan, JP. 1995. *Marketing: contemporary concepts and practices.* 6th edition. Englewood Cliffs, NJ: Prentice Hall, p 119.

Validity and reliability should always be considered in questionnaire development. **Validity** is a measurement instrument's ability to measure what it is supposed to measure. **Reliability** is a measurement instrument's ability to produce essentially identical results after repeated use.

Pretesting of the questionnaire is essential if the researcher is to be satisfied that the questionnaire designed will perform its various functions.[26] The questionnaire is tested on a small sample of respondents to identify and eliminate potential problems; it helps reveal errors while they can still be easily corrected. It should be tried out on a selected group similar in composition to the one that will ultimately be sampled.

When the questionnaire has been designed, a decision must be made on how to contact the survey participants. Survey research data can be obtained from mail, via e-mail, telephone or personal interview. Figure 3.8 shows the relative advantages and disadvantages of mail, telephone and personal surveys. These three types of surveys are now discussed.

- *Mail survey*. For mail surveys, a questionnaire is mailed to possible respondents, and the completed questionnaire is returned by mail to the researcher. Mail surveys are flexible in their application and relatively low in cost, but the major disadvantage is the problem of non-response error. When the geographical area to be covered is large, time is not a major factor, and the questionnaire is relatively short, a mail survey is favoured. Respondents can answer at their convenience, and there are no personal interviews to bias the results. Mail and fax questionnaires are particularly versatile in reaching all types of people in remote geographical areas. E-mail is another form of mail survey that is gaining ground; however, its use is limited to those respondents who have e-mail.

- *Telephone survey*. In a telephone survey, an interviewer asks the respondents questions over the telephone. This type of interview is efficient and economical, and, compared to the personal interview, reduces the potential for bias. The basic limitation of the telephone interview relates to the limited amount of data that can be obtained. Technological advances are making telephone surveys less costly and time-consuming; many research firms are working with data entry terminals. The interviewers read the questions off the video screen and enter the respondents' answers on the computer.

- *Personal survey*. In a personal survey the interviewer asks questions of the respondents in a face-to-face situation. The interviewer's task is to contact the respondent, ask the questions, and record the responses.

Face-to-face interviews may cause respondents to bias their responses because of a desire to please or impress the interviewer.

It is also an expensive method involving extensive planning and control. However, the personal interview method renders the best response in most cases.

## FIGURE 3.8 COMPARISON OF MAIL, TELEPHONE AND PERSONAL INTERVIEW SURVEYS

| Criteria | Mail Survey | Telephone Survey | Personal Interview Survey |
|---|---|---|---|
| Cost (assuming a good response rate) | Often lowest | Usually in-between | Usually highest |
| Ability probe | No personal contact or observation | Elaborate on questions, but no personal observation | Observe and probe |
| Respondent able to complete at own convenience | Yes | No | Perhaps, if interview time is prearranged |
| Interviewer bias | No chance | Some, because of voice inflection, etc. | Greatest chance |
| Ability to decide who in the household responds | Least | Some | Greatest |
| Sampling problems | Lack of accurate mailing lists; low response rates | Lack of accurate phone subscriber list; no phone; refusals | Not-at-homes; refusals |
| Impersonality | Greatest | Lack of face-to-face contact | Least |
| Complex questions | Least suitable | Somewhat suitable | Most suitable |
| Visual aids in survey | Little opportunity | No opportunity | Greatest opportunity |
| Opportunity for building rapport | Least | Some | Greatest |
| Potential negative respondent reaction | 'Junk mail' | 'Junk calls' | Invasion of privacy |
| Time lag between soliciting and receiving response | Greatest | Least | |
| Suitable types of questions | Simple, yes-no and multiple-choice questions | Some opportunity for open-ended questions | Greatest opportunity for open-ended questions |
| Requirement for technical skills in conducting interview | Least | Medium | Greatest |

Source: Schoell, W.F and Guiltinan, JP. 1995. *Marketing: contemporary concepts and practices*. 6th edition. Englewood Cliffs, NJ: Prentice Hall, p 116

## INTERNET SURVEYS

In an Internet survey, respondents are recruited over the Internet from potential respondent databases developed by the research firm or via conventional means. Specific target individuals may be contacted by telephone or mail and asked to access a particular Web location to complete the survey.

The survey has certain similarities to a mail survey in terms of its basic advantages and disadvantages. However, in the cyber survey there is the potential for interactivity and the ability to expose respondents to various stimuli (for example, print advertisements, audio for radio advertisements, product and packaging designs and so on). Cyber surveys have the following advantages: speed, cost-effectiveness, broad geographic scope, accessibility and tracking. However, there may be sample control problems with Internet surveys.

## Step 7: Determine the extent of the formal investigation

In this step, the extent of the formal investigation must be determined. This focuses on the design of the *sampling plan*. Sampling involves selecting representative units from a total population. Marketers can predict the reactions of a total market or market segment by systematically focusing on a limited number of units. This is called *sampling*. However, we must first clarify some of the terms which are relevant to sampling.

The group that the marketer is interested in knowing something about is referred to as the *population* or *universe*. Sometimes a population is small enough that a marketer or researcher may study all of the members of the population in order to learn whatever it is they are interested in establishing.[27] In such cases, the whole population or universe can be investigated.

When the population or universe is extremely large, it may be more convenient to study a subset of the population, called a *sample*. A sample is therefore a set of items, called *units*, selected from the population. In the above examples, Corolla owners and every individual household in Soweto represent sampling units.

## EXAMPLES OF A CENSUS

- A study on the marketing knowledge of supermarket retailers who are members of Nafcoc revealed that only 200 Nafcoc members were supermarket retailers. Since this population was relatively small, all of the members were studied and this was a census.

- Suppose Toyota SA wanted to survey people in the country who bought Corollas during the last three years to assess their opinions about the car. The marketing manager could obtain a list of the names of these people rather easily. Each buyer could then be surveyed – most likely by mail. Since this particular survey would include all people in the population, it would be a complete enumeration, or census of the population.

## EXAMPLES OF A SAMPLE

- If the expenditure of households in Soweto is being researched, the researcher may include all the households in Soweto, in which case a census is taken (the sum total of all households in Soweto). However, the researcher may also decide to interview only some of these households, for example, 10% of the households, which is termed a sample.

- A shoe manufacturer who wanted to study the brand preferences of *all* teenagers between 13 and 16 years found it almost impossible to research all these teenagers and decided to draw a sample of 2 500 teenagers.

Also important is a list from which sample units are drawn for the sample, which contains all of the elements in the population being studied. This list is known as the **sample frame**. The survey on Corolla owners, for example, would not be very representative if only those owners in Gauteng were selected for the research.

The **sample** size involves the number of units that are included in the investigation. No fixed rules exist concerning the number of units to be included. However, there are general norms and guidelines in this regard. Samples which are applied in consumer research can often be less than

1% of the population, on condition that a probability sample and statistical formulae are used. In the case of industrial research, however, larger samples are used because the number of industrial clients is considerably smaller than in the case of final consumers.

In this step of the research process a decision is needed about the type of sample. A good sampling plan will produce a sample that is representative of the characteristics of the population from which it is drawn. Two basic types of samples are probability (random) samples and non-probability (non-random) samples.

- ■ *A probability (or random) sample* is a selection in which each item in a population has a known chance of being included through strict statistical procedures. It is the best way to ensure a representative sample. The following random sampling methods can be employed: simple random sampling, stratified random sampling and cluster sampling.[28]

  - – *Simple random sampling* involves the same principle as taking numbers at random from a hat. A detailed listing of the population is needed, as the units are identified by number.

---

### A SIMPLE RANDOM SAMPLE

To draw a simple random sample of ten flats from a block of flats, the researcher should incorporate the flat numbers into a list of the total population (all flats). Flat numbers will then be drawn at random until the prescribed sample size has been reached.

---

  - – In the case of *stratified random sampling,* the population is divided into mutually exclusive subgroups (strata) on the basis of common characteristics. The basis used for stratification (for example, age, income, occupation and gender) must be a characteristic relevant to the research project.

  - – In *cluster sampling* the procedure is different. Simple random sampling treats each population element individually, while stratified sampling treats elements in groups of the population individually. In the case of cluster sampling, the population will be grouped into clusters, and only some of the groups will be randomly selected for study.

The grouping of clusters is done according to ease or availability and should be heterogeneous (different) within subgroups and externally homo- geneous (similar).

## STRATIFIED RANDOM SAMPLING

Suppose you were studying leisure activities of people in the population and you believed that age was relevant. You would stratify the population by age. People in a particular stratum would be of similar ages, but each stratum would differ from the others with respect to age. You could then use simple random sampling to select sampling units from each stratum. Clearly you would need more information on the population to select a stratified sample than to select a simple sample.

■ **Non-probability (or non-random)** sample. This is a selection in which not every item in a population has a known chance of being included because researcher judgement enters into the selection. The sample's representativeness depends on how good the researcher's judgement is. Non-probability sampling can take two forms: convenience sampling and judgement sampling. In the case of **convenience sampling** the sampling units are chosen simply on the basis of convenience, for example:

## CONVENIENCE SAMPLING

Convenience sampling is used in the case of on-the-street interviews, for example, asking people in a supermarket their opinions about a new brand of detergent, and conducting taste tests on cheese with supermarket customers. People who are not at the same place as the interviewer, and people who are not in that particular supermarket at the time when opinions or taste reactions are being sought, do not have a chance of being included in the sample.

In the case of **judgement sampling,** units are chosen on the basis of the researcher's opinion as to their representativeness.

> ### JUDGEMENT SAMPLING
>
> Examples of judgement sampling include selecting a sample of salespeople for their opinions as input to preparing a sales forecast and selecting cities in which to test market new products. The representativeness of these samples depends on the researcher's judgement in selecting the sampling units.

### Step 8: Selecting, training and controlling the interviewers

In this step of the marketing research process, the research design is implemented, that is, the data are collected. Data collection is often the most expensive aspect of the research process and the possibility of error is high. Interviewers thus have to be carefully selected, trained and an important control task has to be performed.

In the **selection** of interviewers it is advisable to establish specific selection criteria. The criteria will depend on the nature of the questionnaire, the type of respondent who is interviewed and factors relating specifically to the investigation. For example, for open questions which require probing, experienced interviewers are required.

Interviewers need to be **trained** to ensure that they all administer the questionnaire in the same manner so that the data can be collected uniformly.[29] The training should cover making the initial contact, asking the questions, probing, recording the answers and terminating the interview.

**Control** of the interviewers should be exercised continuously. The potential for error in data collection is very high. To help ensure that the research design is being implemented correctly, the researcher must monitor and control every phase of its implementation. In a personal interview survey, for example, it is important to monitor the fieldwork. The researcher might take a sample of completed questionnaires and call the respondents to verify that they were, in fact, interviewed.

> ### TRAINING INTERVIEWERS
>
> In a research investigation into the marketing knowledge of supermarket retailers, the interviewers were given instructions as follows:
>
> ■ Speak to the store owner/manager/person in charge of the store upon entering the store.

- Identify yourself.

- Explain what you are doing.

- Hand the respondent the letter of introduction or read it aloud, if necessary.

- Complete the front page (name of store, owner, and so on ).

- Ask all the questions.

- Record responses by following the instruction below each question – for example, tick more than one item, if necessary.

- Do not influence the respondent when asking the questions.

## Step 9: Fieldwork

The information is now actually being collected from the respondents. Various problems may occur during the interviewing process, such as non-response error and respondent and interviewer bias, which are now discussed in more detail.

- **Non-response error**. The researcher's main concern is non-response error, which is caused by respondents who are not at home when the interviewer calls and respondents who refuse to participate in the survey. There is a likelihood that those people might have systematically responded to questions differently from those who did participate in the survey. Thus the researcher wants to ensure that follow-up calls are made in the case of not-at-homes and that interviewers encourage all those on whom they call to participate.

- **Respondent bias**. The interviewer should do his\her best to obtain answers that are honest and as accurate as possible. Some respondents may be inclined to pre-empt the interviewer by providing answers that they think the interviewer is looking for. This bias should be addressed when the interviewer is trained.

- **Interviewer bias**. Interviewer bias can take many forms, for example his/her tone of voice, age, gender or way of interviewing may unconsciously result in bias. Conscious interviewer bias can also occur. For example, the interviewers may complete the questionnaires themselves. This type of interviewer bias can be limited by thorough training, selecting highly motivated interviewers and by exercising strict control during the fieldwork.

### Step 10:   Data processing

When the fieldwork has been completed, the data must be processed. Data processing entails editing and coding the collected data to facilitate analysis. Editors go through completed questionnaires to eliminate those answered by the wrong respondents and to check for readability of the responses. Editing also involves setting up categories for the data in accordance with the research design. Coding assigns the data to proper categories as explained in the box below:

## CATEGORIES FOR DATA

For example, in a survey of cigarette smokers to determine brand usage, the categories might consist of brands, types of cigarettes (filtered, unfiltered, menthol), city size, household income and gender of respondent.

Proper categories for the brands may include:

■ Stuyvesant 20s might be coded brand number 1.

■ Satin Leaf Lights 30s might be coded brand number 2.

Proper categories for the cities may include:

■ Cities consisting of 20 000 people or less might be coded city size number 1.

■ Cities with 1 million or more people, number 5, and so on.

Sometimes questionnaires are precoded by printing the codes on the questionnaires to assist data entry terminal personnel in entering responses directly from the questionnaire. Data processing activities are usually done by means of computers. Thus the data are often put into a computer-readable form and then read into a computer file and stored.

*Data analysis* is done next. Data analysis techniques should be planned in advance of data collection as part of the research design. For example, more data might be collected if computers are used than if the analysis is done manually.

Data analysis involves descriptive analysis – describing responses, calculating averages and so on – in order to transform raw data into an understandable form for the subsequent interpretation of the data. *Tabulation* involves arranging the data in a table, graph or other summary format to facilitate interpretation.

More sophisticated data analysis techniques may also be used as the researcher moves beyond the description of the data to complex statistical analysis of them. Cross-tabulations are often used to show how one variable relates to another.

For example, two-way tabulations provide answers to such questions as 'What is the relationship between gender and brand loyalty in the motorcar market?'

## STATISTICS ON THE INTERNET

There is a tremendous amount of statistical information and advice available over the Internet. The Web is becoming a very useful source of information for the selection of appropriate statistical techniques for a particular problem, the proper use of different statistical techniques, and emerging statistical techniques. In addition, news and special-interest groups can be an excellent source of information and advice regarding the proper use of statistical procedures.

### Step 11: Communicating information to the decision maker

The final step in the research process involves interpreting the findings and communicating this information to the marketing manager. Communication problems between researchers and marketing managers often arise due to their different backgrounds and work environments. Inevitably, the written research report is the document that management will use as its information source in making a decision. Figure 3.9 shows a part of a research report by Markinor.

## FIGURE 3.9   RESULTS OF MARKINOR'S 'BRAND OLD, BRAND NEW' SURVEY

| Most admired companies/businesses (Whites, Coloureds and Indians) | | | Most admired companies/businesses (Blacks) | | |
|---|---|---|---|---|---|
| Company/Business | Rank | Mention | Company/Business | Rank | Mention |
| Pick 'n Pay | 1 | 27,3% | Coca-Cola | 1 | 30,2% |
| Santam | 2 | 15,7% | SA Breweries | 2 | 23,8% |
| Woolworths | 3 | 14,0% | OK Bazaars | 3 | 12,0% |
| Old Mutual | 4 | 12,0% | Toyota | 4 | 11,6% |
| Coca-Cola | 5 | 11,4% | Eskom | 5 | 11,2% |
| Anglo American | 6 | 9,5% | Lever Bros | 6 | 10,7% |
| Edgars | 7 | 9,3% | Pick 'n Pay | 7 | 9,8% |
| Toyota | 8 | 9,0% | Telkom | 8 | 7,3% |
| Volkswagen | 9 | 8,7% | Volkswagen | 9 | 6,9% |
| Standard Bank | 10 | 8,1% | Shell | 10 | 6,6% |
| SA Breweries | 11 | 7,4% | FNB | 11 | 5,2% |
| FNB | 12 | 6,2% | Anglo American | 12 | 5,1% |
| Telkom | 13 | 5,5% | BMW | 13 | 5,0% |
| OK Bazaars | 14 | 5,2% | Edgars | 14 | 4,9% |
| Eskom | 15 | 5,1% | Checkers | 15 | 4,7% |

Source: *Marketing Mix*, November/December 1994, p 66.

In the research report, the problem situation is defined, and the information from secondary and primary sources analysed and interpreted. Conclusions and recommendations are then made. It is not the researcher's task to make decisions or to implement them – that is the task of marketing management. The research objectives must be directly addressed in the report. The use of graphics is highly recommended, as most managers do not have the time to go through complex tables to reach a conclusion.

The researcher should be selective in the amount of information supplied in the research report. It is advisable to publish all the detailed tabulation and statistical calculations in a separate technical report.

## PUBLISHING RESEARCH REPORTS ON THE INTERNET

Some companies and some research companies publish marketing research reports on the Internet. Publishing these reports has become extremely easy because all the latest versions of the major word processing, presentation graphics and spreadsheet packages (for example, Microsoft Office and Lotus Smart Suite) are easy to use.

Publishing reports on the Internet provides qualified users worldwide instant access to these documents. Users can view the marketing research reports on screen and also have full access to supporting audio, video and animation features. They can save the reports for future reference or for more careful analysis at a later stage. Complete reports or portions of reports can be printed out in hard copy if desired.

## 3.5 MARKET POTENTIAL AND SALES FORECASTING

In this last section of the chapter we deal with a specific element of marketing information, namely market potential and sales forecasting. This is a very specialised field, and therefore we will look at only some basic concepts and procedures.[30]

When an enterprise observes a new market trend, based on the information obtained from marketing research or the marketing information system, it is essential that the current size and future potential of the new market demand be determined. Knowledge of market sizes and probable growth patterns provide the basis for the selection of attractive markets and would thus help in the formulation of appropriate marketing strategies for those markets.

The extent to which plans can be successfully implemented depends not only on managers' abilities in setting and implementing strategies but more fundamentally on their ability to predict the market accurately. This means two things: firstly, assessing the market potential, that is, working out how big the total market is, and, secondly, forecasting sales, that is, calculating how big a slice of that market the organisation can obtain .

*Market potential* focuses on the current size and characteristics of the market, whereas *sales forecasting* looks at the future market situation.

### 3.5.1 Levels of market measurement

The size of a market (in other words, the potential or demand) can be measured on different levels, and it is important to clearly    state beforehand what type of market is involved. Market measurement can be determined by consumer level, product level, geographic level and time level. Marketing managers must clearly define the required level of measurement as this would impact directly on the formulation of resulting marketing decision making. Consider the following example (Figure 3.10) of the possible levels of market measurement for Coca-Cola.

### FIGURE 3.10 POSSIBLE LEVELS OF MARKET MEASUREMENT FOR COCA-COLA

| CONSUMER LEVELS | PRODUCT LEVELS | GEOGRAPHIC LEVELS | TIME LEVELS |
|---|---|---|---|
| ■ Schools | ■ All sales of soft drinks in the RSA | ■ Cape metropolitan area | ■ Monthly |
| ■ Defence service | ■ Sales of Coca-Cola | ■ KwaZulu-Natal | ■ Seasonally |
| ■ Fitness fanatics | ■ Sales of Diet Coke | ■ RSA | ■ Annually |
| ■ Sports meetings | ■ Sales of Tab | ■ Southern Africa | |

- **Consumer level**. The consumer level of demand measurement is the most popular level used as it provides information on the number of final consumers defined in different market segments. Coca-Cola would, for example, be interested in the demand for Coke in schools, at sports meetings and among fitness fanatics.

- **Product level**. On the product level, an enterprise can measure consumer demand for one brand or for all of its brands in a given product category. As most markets are targeted by various formats of the same product, the demand measurement can be expressed in terms of the total number of current buyers for each product type. Coca-Cola, for example, would be interested in the sales of all soft drinks in the RSA, sales of Coca-Cola, sales of Diet Coke, sales of Tab and so on.

- **Geographic level**. On the geographic level, the total market can be divided into geographical segments and it is thus possible to express the demand measurement in geographic terms. Coca-Cola may be interested in certain areas such as the Cape metropolitan area, KwaZulu-Natal, the RSA, and southern Africa.

■ *Time level*. A demand measurement should also be specific in terms of the time of purchase and should provide information on the sales over different time periods. Coca-Cola may be interested in monthly sales, seasonal sales and annual sales.

### 3.5.2  Relevant markets for measurement

The different types of markets which can be measured are not all relevant to a specific enterprise. It depends on whether the enterprise is actively involved or interested in the particular market. It is thus necessary to distinguish the relevant markets that can be used in estimating market potential:

■ *Total market* (also referred to as the market potential) pertains to all actual and potential buyers of a product type, if it is generally available and offered for purchase, and whether consumers have the ability to buy. For example, the total market for Coke is the RSA in total.

■ *Available market* refers only to those actual and potential buyers of a product who have the interest, income and ability to buy the product at a particular point in time (for example, metropolitan areas where consumers are able to buy the product because of its availability and their level of income).

■ *Target market* is that part of the available market to which the company has chosen to direct its marketing activities (for example, the 16 to 35 year-old age group). The target market for Coke may include only those parts of the metropolitan population that fall into particular age groups and lifestyle categories.

■ *Penetrated market* refers to the number of consumers who have already bought the product. Coke's penetrated market refers to that section of the target market that has already bought the product.

### 3.5.3  Market and sales potential

We first need to clarify the concepts 'market potential' and 'sales potential' before we look at ways of estimating or measuring market and sales potential.

■ *Market potential*. Market potential is concerned with what is possible, in other words, it focuses on the current size of the market. Market potential is '*the maximum possible sales of a specific product in a specific market over a specific period for all sellers in the industry*'.

It assumes that all sellers are presenting their maximum marketing effort under a given set of environmental conditions. Market potential thus sets an upper limit for industry sales. This definition of market potential raises problems in calculating a figure for market potential, as it involves many assumptions about competitors and the environment and because it needs a precise definition of 'the market.' In addition, methods of quantifying the variables concerned are also required.

## MARKET POTENTIAL FOR BEER

Market potential in the beer industry can refer to one or more of the following markets:

- Total sales of beer.
- Total sales of a particular form of beer (light, dark).
- An entire market.
- Only a segment of that market.

A segment, in turn, can be defined in terms of any of the segmentation variables, for example the market potential in city A only could be estimated. Alternatively, we could estimate market potential within a certain age or income segment of people in city A.

Market potential data help in evaluating which opportunities the marketer should pursue, for example, in determining which market segments to target. Such data also help in deciding the level of marketing effort that should be committed to the various segments and in providing benchmarks for evaluating performance in selected segments.

## THE TOY INDUSTRY REVIEWING ITS DEFINITION OF THE MARKET[31]

In the early 1990s, the traditional toy industry was reviewing its definition of the market following a report that children are leaving the traditional toy market earlier and earlier, and that their needs, wants and consumption choices are broadening. This means that toy manufacturers are competing directly with clothing, trainers, videos, electronic games and so on, for children's disposable income. The toy manufacturers now have to consider themselves in the youth gift market, not just the toy market.

- **Sales potential.** Even after the potential has been estimated for the market as a whole (market potential), a company will then need to determine its own sales potential, that is, the share of the market that it could reasonably capture. Sales potential is '**the upper limit of sales that a firm could possibly reach for a specific product in a specific market over a specific time period**'. It is based on a maximum level of marketing effort and an assumed set of environmental conditions. A company's sales potential, therefore, is the share of market potential that it might capture if it maximised its marketing effort. Sales potential is therefore partly a result of the company's marketing effort and its success in attracting and holding customers.

Having a clear idea of market and sales potential provides a useful input to the marketing planning process. It is especially important for planning selling efforts and allocating resources. The allocation of salesforce effort, and the establishment of distribution point and service support centres, for example, can reflect sales potential rather than actual sales, thus allowing scope for expansion. Similarly, sales potential can also be used to plan sales territories, quotas, salesforce compensation and targets for prospecting.

### 3.5.4  Estimating market and sales potential

The methods used for estimating market and sales potential depend on how new or innovative the product or service is, and how mature the market is. We distinguish between the breakdown methods and build-up methods.

- **Breakdown methods.** The most common breakdown method used to estimate market and sales potential is **total market measurement**. The total market measurement begins with any total industry or market data that may be available from secondary research. This information is then broken down to market segment level and thereafter to the company's own sales potential. This method relies heavily on the availability of a long series of data on industry sales volume and consumption by segments within that market, but rarely are such complete and detailed data available. Potential is thus often estimated from what data are available and then adjusted to take account of the current marketing environment. Once market and segment potentials have been established, sales potential can be derived by estimating competitors' relative market shares and then calculating how those might change as a result of expected actions, for example a new product launch.

- **Build-up methods**. There are three main methods for estimating reliable market and sales potential figures: census, survey, and secondary data. The **census method** is based on a detailed consideration of every buyer and potential buyer in a market. This may be difficult in mass consumer markets, but is more feasible in industrial situations. The market potential is effectively the sum of all the potentials estimated for individual purchasers.

  - The **survey method** is more widely used in consumer markets where a representative sample of consumers is asked about purchase intentions. This information can then be used as a basis for calculating total market or sales potential. The main problem, however, is that respondents might not tell the truth about their intentions.

  - **Secondary data** can be used to establish sales and market potential. Internal sales records can be used to predict individual customers' purchasing on the basis of past behaviour. In this approach, the sales potentials are produced first and the market potential is then derived from those figures.

## 3.5.5 Market and sales forecasting

The terms 'market forecast' and 'sales forecast' must be defined before we consider the development of a sales forecast.

- **Market forecast**. A market forecast is '*an estimate of the expected sales of a specific product in a specific market over a specific time period for all sellers in the industry*'.

  It is based on an expected level of industry effort and an expected set of environmental conditions. In other words, the market forecast is the portion of market potential that is expected to be realised.

- **Sales forecast**. A sales forecast is '*an estimate of the number of units a firm expects to reach for a specific product in a specific market over a specific time period*'. It is based on an intended level and type of marketing effort by the company and an expected set of environmental conditions.

Marketing often plays a central role in preparing and disseminating forecasts.

This is perhaps one of its most important functions, as the sales and market forecasts provided are the basis of all subsequent planning and decision making within most areas of the company.

### EXAMPLES OF FORECASTS

- A car manufacturer wanting to forecast the demand for each model in the product line.

- A tour operator wanting to forecast the demand for specific destinations.

- A university wanting to forecast numbers of full-time, part-time and overseas students by programme offered by the university.

The forecast is the starting point for all subsequent decisions. If this is not done correctly, the whole company can encounter major capacity or cash-flow problems.

### SOME PROBLEMATIC FORECASTING SITUATIONS

- In fashion markets it can be very difficult to forecast what styles are going to sell and in what quantities, hence the popularity of 'end of season' sales as retailers try to sell off surplus stock.

- Holiday companies and airlines also find forecasting difficult, and again find themselves selling off surplus holidays or seats on aircraft at discounted rates. This occurs until actual departure dates.

There is no such thing as a rigid or absolute forecast. Different forecasters using different forecasting methods are almost certain to reach different results. Forecasts should, however, share some common characteristics. They should:

- be based upon historical information from which a projection can be made;

- look forward over a specific, clearly defined time period; and

- make clearly specified assumptions, since uncertainty characterises the future.

## 3.5.6  Forecasting methods

There are several forecasting methods. Rather than relying on only one method, planners often use a number of methods. We will briefly consider the salesforce survey, expert survey and time series analysis.

- **Salesforce surveys** can provide a wealth of information. Such surveys involve asking sales representatives to provide forecasts on customers, dealers, accounts and so on. The salesforce is a valuable source of expert opinion, since representatives are very close to customers on a daily basis and will learn of likely changes in purchasing intentions early. The main problems of these surveys are bias and naivety.

- **Expert surveys** can be used by bringing outside expertise into the sales forecasting process. The expert survey is the sales forecasting method that involves the participation of people outside the firm who have special knowledge and experience in the market under consideration. This includes economists, consultants and retired executives.

- **Time series analysis** is a means of using historical data to predict the future. Analysis of historic data can reveal patterns in the organisation's sales figures. These patterns include trends, cycles, seasonality and random factors. In the case of **trends**, for example, extrapolation of data on a straight-or curved-line basis can give a broad view of the general direction in which sales are moving. **Cycles** reflect periodic changes in patterns over a period of time. **Seasonality**, that is shorter-term fluctuations around an overall trend, may even be observed on a daily or weekly basis, if that is what the organisation requires. Any forecast must make allowances for **random factors** such as strikes, riots and civil commotion (especially in the insurance industry).

### SUMMARY

In this chapter, we focused firstly on the information needs of marketers and how they gather and use that information to develop marketing strategies. More specifically, we dealt with the marketing information system.

We also looked at the factors involved when a company decides to conduct marketing research and the research techniques available to gather the specific information needed by the company. The steps in the marketing research process were dealt with comprehensively. We also looked at the important role of the Internet in marketing research. Finally, we examined market potential and sales forecasting, a specific element of marketing information.

## REFERENCES

1. Burns, AC and Bush, RF. 1998. *Marketing research*. 2nd edition. Upper Saddle River: Prentice Hall, p 4.

2. Burns and Bush p 4.

3. McDaniel, C and Gates, R. 1998. *Marketing research essentials*. 2nd edition. Cincinnati: South-Western College Publishing, p 5.

4. McDaniel and Gates p 3.

5. Brink, A. 1997. *The marketing perception of grocery store retailers belonging to black business associations in Gauteng*. Unpublished thesis for the DCom degree. Pretoria: Unisa, pp 124-126.

6. Brink pp 134-140.

7. Brink p 143.

8. Schoell, WF and Guiltinan, JP. 1995. *Marketing: contemporary concepts and practices*. 6th edition. Englewood Cliffs, NJ: -Prentice Hall, p   103.

9. Solomon, MR and Stuart, EW. 1997. *Marketing: real people, real choices*. Upper Saddle River: Prentice Hall, p 153.

10. Schoell and Guiltinan p 104.

11. Martins, JH; Loubser, M and Van Wyk, H de J. 1996. *Marketing research: a South African approach*. Pretoria: University of South Africa Press, p 14.

12. Kotler, P and Armstrong, G. 1993. *Marketing: an introduction.* 3rd edition. Englewood Cliffs, NJ: Prentice Hall, p 95.

13. McDaniel and Gates p 26.

14. Strydom, JW (ed). 1998. *Introduction to marketing*. Cape Town: Juta, p 100.

15. McDaniel and Gates p 28.

16. Schoell and Guiltinan p 109.

17. Brink p 250.

18. Strydom p 103.

19. Van der Walt, A; Strydom, JW; Marx, S and Jooste, CJ. 1996. *Marketing management*. Cape Town: Juta, p 152.

20. Schoell and Guiltinan p 115.

21. Strydom p 104.

22. Burns and Bush pp 216-217.

23. Brink p 252.

24. Brink p 253.

25. Schoell and Guiltinan p 119.

26. Martins *et al* p 232.

27. Burns and Bush p 67.

28. Van der Walt *et al* pp 154-155.

29. Brink p 261.

30. This section on market potential and sales forecasting is largely based on Brassington, FB and Pettitt, S. 1997. *Principles of marketing*. London: Pitman Publishing; Schoell & Guiltinan; and Van der Walt *et al*.

31. Brassington and Pettitt p 892.

# CHAPTER 4

## CONSUMER AND BUSINESS BEHAVIOUR

## 4.1 INTRODUCTION

The question of why people buy has interested marketing management for many years – what thought process result in the decision to buy or not to buy. Prospective buyers are usually exposed to various sales messages. A person then internalises or considers this information and makes a buying decision.

This process of internalisation is referred to as a 'black box' because we cannot see into a buyer's mind which means that marketing management can apply the stimuli and observe the behaviour of the consumer, but cannot witness the consumer's actual decision-making process. The classic model of buyer.behaviour is called a stimulus-response model (Figure 4.1).

### FIGURE 4.1 STIMULUS-RESPONSE MODEL OF CONSUMER BEHAVIOUR

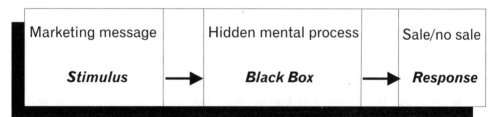

| Marketing message | Hidden mental process | Sale/no sale |
|---|---|---|
| *Stimulus* ➡ | *Black Box* ➡ | *Response* |

A stimulus (advertising message) is applied, resulting in a response (purchase decision). This model assumes that consumers will respond in some predictable manner to the stimuli. Unfortunately, it does not tell us why they buy or do not buy the product. This information is concealed in the black box. Marketing management seeks to understand as much as possible about the mental process that yields the consumers' responses.

This requires a thorough knowledge and understanding of what determines these needs and how consumers respond to satisfy these needs.

The marketer has to have a thorough understanding of consumer behaviour[1]. The field of consumer behaviour studies how individuals, groups and organisations select, buy, use and dispose of goods, services, ideas or experiences to satisfy their needs and desires. Understanding consumer behaviour is not simple. Customers may state their needs and desires but act otherwise. They may respond to influences that change their decisions at the last minute. Marketers must nevertheless study their target consumers' wants, perceptions, shopping and buying behaviour.[2]

While the needs, demands and preferences of each individual are unique, there are also many common or similar behaviour patterns and all consumers follow more or less the same course when decisions must be taken. In decision making, all people are influenced to a greater or lesser extent by the actions of others with whom they come into contact. The unique, inherent qualities of consumers, the phases in the consumer decision-making process, and societal influences are discussed in this chapter.

The behaviour patterns of a typical consumer differ from those of the user of industrial products and services. While a consumer often decides to purchase products for emotional reasons, the industrial consumer only buys those products that are really required in further production processes. In this chapter, a distinction is drawn between consumer behaviour and the behaviour of industrial buyers (business buying behaviour).

## LEARNING OUTCOMES

At the end of this chapter you will be able to:

- describe the individual factors that influence the behaviour of individual consumers;
- explain which group factors can influence consumer behaviour with regard to cultural, peer, reference and family groups;
- analyse, step-by-step, the decision-making process and indicate what happens after a product or service has been purchased;
- indicate how buyers take decisions in the industrial purchasing process; and
- explain how consumer behaviour differs from business buying behaviour.

Marketing management needs extensive information on and knowledge of consumer and buyer behaviour in order to focus the market offering specifically on final consumers or, alternatively, on industrial buyers. Marketing management can, in turn, influence society as the need to own desirable products can motivate consumers to try to improve their lifestyles.

## 4.2 TYPES OF PURCHASE DECISIONS

Consumer decision making varies with the type of purchase decision. Assael[3] distinguished four types of purchase decisions based on the degree of buyer involvement and the degree of difference among brands (Table 4.1).

### TABLE 4.1 Types of purchasing decisions

|  | HIGH INVOLVEMENT | LOW INVOLVEMENT |
|---|---|---|
| Significant differences between brands | Complex purchasing behaviour | Variety-seeking purchasing behaviour |
| Few differences between brands | Dissonance reducing behaviour | Habitual purchasing behaviour |

Source: Adapted from Assael, H. 1987. *Consumer behaviour and marketing action.* Boston: Kent, p 87.

- ■ *Complex purchase behaviour*: Consumers engage in complex purchasing behaviour when they are highly involved in a purchase and aware of significant differences among brands. This is usually the case when the product is expensive, being bought infrequently, involves risk and is self-expressive (for example, motorcars, computers, clothes, furniture and electronic equipment). Buyers need assistance in learning about the product's attributes and benefits.

- ■ *Dissonance reducing behaviour*: Buyers are highly involved in the purchase, but believe that there are few differences between the brands. The buyer will shop around to determine what is available on the market but will buy fairly quickly (for example, lawnmowers and carpets).

- ■ *Habitual purchasing behaviour*: Buyers demonstrate low involvement and significant brand differences are absent.

Buyers buy out of habit but are not brand loyal (for example, salt, milk, bread and deodorants). The products are mostly low cost, frequent purchases.

- ***Variety-seeking purchasing behaviour***: These buying situations are characterised by low consumer involvement but significant brand differences. Consumers do a great deal of brand switching for the sake of variety (for example, take-away food, restaurants, ice cream, entertainment, salad dressing and coffee).[4]

Two further types of decision making also occur:

- ***Routine decision making***: This occurs when a consumer, without consciously thinking about it, consistently purchases the same branded products. This loyalty to specific branded products is the result of the extended decision-making process of the preceding period. Routine purchasing reduces the necessity of repeating the decision-making process each time an item is needed, thereby facilitating the purchasing task. Household necessities which must be re-stocked regularly, such as toiletries, detergents, margarine, coffee and tea, are often purchased on this basis.

- ***Impulsive decision making***: Implies unplanned action, on the spur of the moment, in contrast to the purposeful planning visible in true decision making. This is not completely correct. In impulsive decision making, the consumer also progresses through all the phases of the decision-making process. Usually action follows immediately after the decision has been reached, and to a bystander it seems as though planning (which includes purposefully searching for and evaluating information) did not precede the action. Impulsive action viewed in this light indicates a decision made at the point of purchase and therefore cannot be regarded as an irresponsible approach to purchasing. It can be concluded that decision making is lengthy when the decision is deemed important. Decision making can also occur spontaneously when the consumer impulsively buys immediately after becoming aware of an unsatisfied need.

## 4.3 FACTORS INFLUENCING CONSUMER BEHAVIOUR

Several individual and group factors strongly influence the decision-making process. Figure 4.2 summarises these influences.

## FIGURE 4.2 OVERVIEW OF CONSUMER BEHAVIOUR

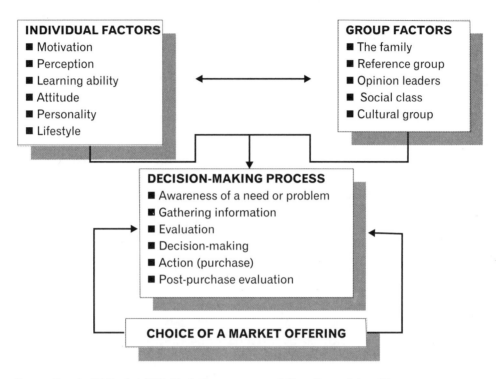

**INDIVIDUAL FACTORS**
- Motivation
- Perception
- Learning ability
- Attitude
- Personality
- Lifestyle

**GROUP FACTORS**
- The family
- Reference group
- Opinion leaders
- Social class
- Cultural group

**DECISION-MAKING PROCESS**
- Awareness of a need or problem
- Gathering information
- Evaluation
- Decision-making
- Action (purchase)
- Post-purchase evaluation

**CHOICE OF A MARKET OFFERING**

Source: Van der Walt, *et al*. 1996. *Marketing management*. Cape Town: Juta, p 77.

### 4.3.1   Individual factors influencing consumer buying decisions

Individual factors refer to factors inherent in human behaviour that will influence an individual's behaviour as a consumer.

#### 4.3.1.1   Motivation

All behaviour starts with needs and wants. ***Needs are the basic forces that motivate an individual to do something. Wants are needs that are learned during an individual's lifetime***. Everyone, for example, needs some kind of liquid to quench their thirst. Some people learned to want mineral water, others a soft drink and others either coffee or tea. A ***motive*** is a need or want that is sufficiently stimulated to move an individual to seek satisfaction. Hunger that is strong enough to move the consumer to seek out a take-away meal, and fear of burglary great enough that the consumer seeks security by installing an alarm system, are examples of aroused needs/wants that become motives for behaviour.[5]

It is sometimes quite easy to identify the motives that underlie a buying decision, while at other times it is impossible to identify these motives. Stanton *et al*.[6] state that buying motives may be grouped into three different levels, depending on the consumer's awareness of them and their willingness to divulge them:

- **Conscious need level:** Consumers know the motives and are quite willing to talk about them.
- **Preconscious need level:** Consumers are aware of the motives but will not reveal them to others.
- **Unconscious need level:** Consumers cannot explain the factors motivating their buying actions because they are unconscious or sub-conscious motives.

To further complicate the situation, a purchase is often the result of multiple motives, some even in conflict with one another. In buying a new car, the young buyer searches for economy and affordability, but also comfort and luxury.

The best known and also the most accepted theory of classifying the diversity of needs is that of Maslow. He classified human needs in a scheme in which the lower-level needs must first be satisfied, or partly satisfied, before the higher-level needs can fully emerge. Figure 4.3 shows Maslow's hierarchy of needs.

The lowest-level needs are physiological, which help to ensure the survival of the individual. The highest level is reflected in the desire for self-actualisation. According to this theory, the individual is motivated to fulfil whichever need is most strongly felt at any given moment.

## FIGURE 4.3 MASLOW'S HIERARCHY OF NEEDS

|  |  |  |  |  |
|--|--|--|--|--|
|  |  |  |  | 5 SELF-ACTUALISATION - self-fulfilment |
|  |  |  | 4 | EGO - prestige, success, self-esteem, status |
|  |  | 3 | SOCIAL - love, friendship, affiliation | |
|  | 2 | SAFETY AND SECURITY - protection, physical well-being | | |
| 1 | PHYSIOLOGICAL - hunger, thirst, sex | | | |

Source: Adapted from Maslow, A. H. 1954. *Motivation and personality*. New York: Harper & Row.

The following motives (human needs) appear in Figure 4.3:

- *A basic physiological need*, hunger, compels the consumer to purchase bread and milk.
- *Safety needs* motivate the consumer to erect a security fence, take out insurance, and to be concerned about his/her health.
- *Social needs* underlie a host of purchasing decisions, from cosmetics to deodorants.
- *Ego needs* cause the consumer to purchase luxury products as symbols of status and success.
- *Self-actualisation* is the highest human need and has to do with personal development and individuality. It is unfortunately true that few people are in a position to satisfy this need. Enrolling for art classes is an example of an attempt to express individuality.

As is the case with physiological and other emotional motives, economic motives also influence consumers to purchase. The economic motives are all rational by nature, dealing with technical functions and performance of a product, and are usually expressed in quantitative terms.

They can also be seen as the functional motives underlying buying behaviour. Physiological, emotional and economic motives are depicted in Figure 4.4.

## FIGURE 4.4 MOTIVES OF CONSUMERS

| PHYSIOLOGICAL MOTIVES | | EMOTIONAL MOTIVES | | ECONOMIC MOTIVES |
|---|---|---|---|---|
| ■ Hunger | | ■ Love | | ■ Efficiency |
| ■ Thirst | | ■ Friendship | | ■ Economy |
| ■ Sex | ←→ | ■ Status | ←→ | ■ Reliability |
| ■ Safety | | ■ Prestige | | ■ Durability |
| | | ■ Esteem | | ■ Convenience |
| | | ■ Self-actualisation | | ■ Quality |

Source: Adapted from Walters, GG. 1978. *Consumer behaviour.* Homewood: Richard D Irwin, p 53.

### 4.3.1.2   Perception

A motive activates behaviour intended to satisfy the aroused need. Since behaviour can take many forms, an individual gathers information from the environment to help in making a choice. The process of receiving, organising and assigning meaning to information or stimuli detected by the five senses is known as **perception**. It is the way that consumers interpret or give meaning to the world surrounding them[7]. The consumer can, for example, form a perception of the quality of a product by feeling it or by just looking at the product.

Perception involves seeing, hearing, feeling, tasting and smelling. Stimuli picked up by the senses are relayed to the brain, where they are interpreted. The consumer reacts according to this interpretation and not always according to the objective reality. Subjective factors always play a role in perception. The experiences, values and prejudices of an individual colour his/her perceptions. This means that few people perceive things in exactly the same way.

---

**SENSORY STIMULI**

- **Seeing** plays a role in purchasing jewellery or fashion clothes.

- **Hearing** plays a role in purchasing musical instruments or electronic equipment.

- **Feeling** plays a role in purchasing material/clothes, fruit and bread.

- **Tasting** plays a role in purchasing sweets, toothpaste or foodstuffs.

- **Smelling** plays a role in purchasing perfume, fresh bread, flowers or deodorants.

In purchasing a new motorcar, virtually all the senses (except taste) play a role in perception.

---

A consumer must pick up sensory stimuli from the environment before he/she will react. Perception also plays a role in the interpretation of a marketing message. A consumer will perceive a certain market offering only after he/she has received sensory stimuli, especially after seeing or hearing the marketing message.

---

Because so many, often conflicting, stimuli are perceived simultaneously, individuals tend to defend themselves. They may ignore or distort the meaning of unwelcome stimuli. Such perceptual defence mechanisms[8] are used to protect a person against undesirable stimuli from the environment, and include the following:

- **Selective exposure** occurs when people selectively choose to expose themselves only to certain stimuli. A consumer can, for example, avoid unwelcome stimuli by quickly paging through a magazine and missing the advertisements or by turning off the radio or television when commercials come on.

- **Selective attention** occurs when the individual does not pay full attention to the stimuli picked up by the senses. Selective attention causes a consumer not to comprehend the content of the marketing message.

- **Selective interpretation** occurs when the stimuli are perceived, but the message itself is not interpreted as it was intended to be. The consumer can interpret the marketing message incorrectly by distorting the meaning or by misunderstanding it.

- **Selective recall** refers to the individual's ability to remember only certain stimuli and to forget others which may be important. At the point of purchase, consumers may have forgotten the advertisement and must therefore once again be reminded to purchase the product (see Figure 4.5).

## FIGURE 4.5 INFORMATION PROCESSING IS SELECTIVE

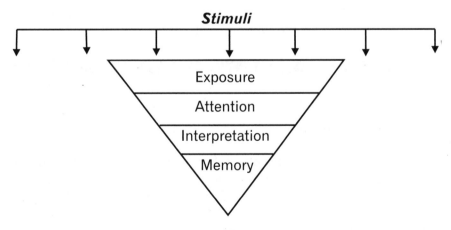

Source: Bennett, JA, Grové, TA and Jooste, C.J. 1995. *Introduction to marketing management.* Johannesburg: RAU internal publication, p 34.

**A MARKETING MANAGER MAY FIND DIFFERENT WAYS TO DEAL WITH THE FOLLOWING:**

**1. SELECTIVE ATTENTION**

- Larger stimuli (one-page advertisements versus fractional advertisements) and higher frequency (the repetition of advertisements on the radio or in different media) will be more likely to be noticed.

- Both colour and movement attract attention.

- Objects placed near the centre of the visual field are more likely to be noticed than those near the edge of the field (eye-level space in supermarkets).

**2. SELECTIVE INTERPRETATION**

- Marketers should carefully pre-test their message to ensure that it is being interpreted correctly.

- Marketers should determine how cultural differences influence the use of colour, symbols and numbers.

- Marketers should not set unrealistic expectations.

**3. SELECTIVE RETENTION**

- Visibility influences the ability to retrieve items from our memory for use in consumption decisions (in this case, it would assist to make use of demonstrations).

- Repetition is important to reinforce the message.

- Make use of the consumer's ability to learn (the result of a combination of motivation, attention, experience and repetition).

Source: Bennet, JA, Grové, TA and Jooste, CJ. 1995. *Introduction to marketing management.* Johannesburg: RAU internal publication, pp 35-36.

### 4.3.1.3 Learning ability

The consumer's ability to learn also influences behaviour. The consumer must, for example, learn which product attributes relate to which brand and where it can be purchased. Consumers must also be able to recognise the distinctive packaging. Consumers must remember the information supplied in the marketing message when they are in a position to purchase the product.

*Learning can be defined as the result of a combination of motivation, attention, experience and repetition.* Three elements are implied in this definition. In order to learn, the learner/consumer must be **motivated**, must give **full attention** to the message (must perceive and experience it), and there must be some measure of effective **repetition**. A considered combination of these three elements results in a successful learning situation. Imbalance in any way invariably leads to failure[9].

The following learning principles are important when formulating marketing messages:

- Repetition is important to reinforce the message.

- A unique message is best remembered.

- A message which is easy to understand is easy to learn.

- The law of **primac**y states that the aspect mentioned at the beginning of the message is best remembered, but according to the law of **recency**, the last-mentioned aspect is best remembered.

- Demonstrations facilitate the learning process.

- Promises of rewards (or threats of punishment) facilitate learning.

- Serious fear-producing messages are avoided; consumers tend to distort such messages.

### 4.3.1.4  Attitude

*An attitude is a positive or negative feeling about an object (for example, a brand, product or company) that predisposes a person to behave in a particular way toward that object*[10]. Attitudes also encompass an individual's value system, which represents personal standards of good and bad, right and wrong, and so forth[11].

### NEGATIVE ATTITUDES TO PRODUCTS

- Conservationists abhor killing wild animals and maintain a very negative attitude to the wearing of fur coats.

- Members of some religious groups disapprove of the use of cosmetics or beef or pork.

- Conservative people exhibit a negative attitude towards way-out fashions. They often forbid their children to purchase these fashions.

- Some men may have negative attitudes towards using diet soft drinks which they believe are targeted primarily at women.

All attitudes have the following in common[12]:

- Attitudes are learned through previous experience with a product or indirect experiences such as reading about the product or interaction with social groups.
- Attitudes related to an object – consumers can hold attitudes only about something and attitudes will vary from object to object.
- Attitudes have direction and intensity. Attitudes toward the object are either favourable or unfavourable. The consumer either likes or dislikes diet soft drinks. The strength of their liking or disliking can also differ – some customers may like the object more than others.
- Attitudes tend to be stable – once formal, attitudes usually endure, and the longer they are held, the more resistant to change they become.

Marketers strive to reinforce positive attitudes held by consumers. The Toyota Camry is seen as a family, spacious and economical car. The advertising campaign reinforces these attitudes by emphasising the boot space or the fact that three children can comfortably fit on the back seat.

It is far more difficult to change strongly held attitudes. When a marketer is faced with negative or unfavourable attitudes, there are options to[13]:

- Change the consumer's beliefs about the attributes or brands, for example, the campaign to promote red meat as healthy meat is endorsed by the Heart Foundation.
- Change the importance of beliefs. For years, consumers have known that bran cereals are high in natural fibre. Today, however, these cereals are promoted as a possible factor in preventing certain types of cancer.
- Add new beliefs, for example, that a particular toothpaste not only prevents tooth decay but also whitens teeth, or washing powder that brightens the colour of a garment.

## 4.3.1.5 Personality

Personality refers to those *psychological characteristics of people which both determine and reflect their reaction to environmental influences*.

Personality distinguishes one individual from another, and one group of individuals with similar characteristics from another group[14]. There are several personality types identified by research.

While research seems to indicate that individual traits are not good predictors of behaviour, it is a well-known fact that marketers use personality traits to describe individuals and to differentiate between them. See Table 4.2 for an example of traits. It is also true that marketers can expect that consumers will tend to purchase the product that best suits their personality. Mercedes-Benz drivers are, for example, perceived to be more conservative than BMW users, who are perceived to be far more aggressive and assertive.

## TABLE 4.2 Examples of personality traits

| | | |
|---|---|---|
| RESERVED (critical, stiff) | vs | OUTGOING (warm-hearted, participating) |
| HUMBLE (stable, mild) | vs | ASSERTIVE (aggressive, competitive) |
| SELF-ASSURED (secure, complacent) | vs | APPREHENSIVE (insecure, troubled, worrying) |
| RELAXED (tranquil, composed) | vs | TENSE (frustrated) |
| EXPEDIENT (disregard rules) | vs | CONSCIENTIOUS (persistent, moralistic) |
| DEPENDENT (follower) | vs | SELF-SUFFICIENT(resourceful, independent) |
| UNDISCIPLINED (lax, careless) | vs | CONTROLLED (willpower, precise, comprehensive) |

Source: Hawkins, D; Best, RJ and Coney, KA. 1995. *Consumer behaviour*. Chicago. Richard and Irwin, p 310.

### 4.3.1.6 Lifestyle

*Lifestyle refers to the way of living of individuals or families*. The lifestyle concept provides descriptions of behaviour and purchasing patterns, especially the ways in which people spend their time and money. Personality, motives and attitudes also influence lifestyle.

The AIO classification describes lifestyle according to the activities, interests and opinions of consumers. Figure 4.6 indicates some dimensions of lifestyle which can be used to describe the attributes of a specific market segment. Market segmentation is discussed in Chapter 5.

## FIGURE 4.6 LIFESTYLE DIMENSIONS

| ACTIVITIES | | INTERESTS | | OPINIONS |
|---|---|---|---|---|
| Work | | Family | | About the self |
| Hobbies | | Home | | Social problems |
| Holidays | ←→ | Work | ←→ | Politics |
| Entertainment | | Sport | | Economy |
| Purchasing | | Food | | Education |
| Sport | | Media | | Products |
| Club membership | | Own performance | | The future |

Source: Van der Walt, A. *et al*. 1996. *Marketing management*. Cape Town: Juta, p 83.

### 4.3.2  Group factors influencing consumer buying decisions

The consumer is a human being who needs to be affiliated with other groups in the social environment in order to satisfy social needs. Group norms will therefore influence the individual's behaviour patterns. These norms include habits, rules and regulations.

Sanctions (rewards or punishment) are used in formal and informal ways to ensure conformity to norms. Rewards such as social acceptance and approval encourage a person to conform to the prescribed norms of behaviour. Sanctions (such as ostracism) are usually regarded as a very serious punishment by most people. Subtle threats of this nature are often included in advertisements for toothpaste, deodorants and skin lotions, the implication being that the person not using these products is in danger of being ridiculed, held in contempt or ostracised.

Considering the fact that an individual can belong to many different groups (all of which maintain distinctive norms of behaviour), one can appreciate the degree of social pressure placed on the economic activities of an individual. There are very few products that are without any social significance at all, and usually a consumer succumbs to the pressure of social needs. The different groups that can compel a consumer to conform to group norms are the cultural group, the family, reference groups and option leaders[15].

### 4.3.2.1  Culture

*Culture* comprises a complex system of values, norms and symbols which have developed in society over a period of time and in which all its members share. The cultural values, norms and symbols are created by people and are transmitted from one generation to another to ensure survival and also to facilitate adaptation to the circumstances of life. They are transmitted from parents to children. In this process, the school, church and other social institutions also play an important role (this process is referred to as *socialisation*).

Each cultural group comprises several subcultures, each with its own norms, values and symbols. There are four main subcultures, categorised according to nationality, religion, race and geographical area of residence. Besides the four main groups, smaller subcultures can develop, perhaps according to language, age, interests or occupation[16].

South African society is fragmented into many cultural groups and subgroups. Although whites are not numerically dominant, their norms, values and symbols do exert influence on economic activity. Most advertisements therefore reflect Western culture. Advertising messages are directed simultaneously at the black and white consumer markets and are often variations of the same theme. Marketing management must, however, be careful not to use symbols which can be interpreted incorrectly (or differently), and not to portray unacceptable behaviour patterns. Effective communication can take place only if the theme of the advertising message reflects the cultural norms, values and symbols of the cultural group to which it is directed.

### 4.3.2.2 Family[17]

Of all the groups influencing consumer behaviour, the individual maintains the closest contact with the family. In family interaction, the child learns behaviour patterns by means of the socialisation process.

The family can be regarded as a nuclear group whose members live in close contact with one another and act as a decision-making unit when they attempt to satisfy individual needs from one shared source (the family income). This fact implies that individual needs must necessarily be subordinated to those of other members to a greater or lesser extent. This leads to consultation and joint decision making among family members.

With regard to the influence of the family, there are two aspects which are of importance to the enterprise in developing its marketing strategy: the family life cycle and role differentiation between family members. The family life-cycle phases are as follows:

- **Newly-wed phase**. Both members of this unit are usually economically active and pool their incomes, which means they can usually afford to buy durables and even luxuries.
- **Phase of family growth**. This phase starts with the arrival of the first child in the relationship, and markedly changes previous consumer behaviour patterns.
- **Maturity phase**. The children in the family have reached the adolescent stage where, in addition to their basic needs, they have also developed their own norms, preferences and lifestyles.
- **Post-parental phase**. All the children have left home and the parents spend proportionally less on basic household necessities. They have greater disposable income to spend on luxuries.
- **Sole survivor**. The consumption patterns and the lifestyle of the surviving spouse change drastically.

Role differentiation and the influences exerted by family members on consumer decision making in the family are depicted in Figure 4.7.

## FIGURE 4.7  ROLE DIFFERENTIATION IN CONSUMER DECISION MAKING IN THE FAMILY

| ROLES | FAMILY MEMBERS |
|---|---|
| The *initiator* is the person who makes the first suggestion regarding products to be purchased. | Teenagers often act as initiators, for example, requesting a soft drink or ice-cream. |
| The *influencer* is the person who implicity or explicity influences the final decision because this person's suggestions and wishes are reflected in the ultimate decision made by the family. | Children's preferences (for example, for a certain kind of breakfast cereal) influence family decision making. |
| The *decision maker* is the person who actually chooses between alternatives and makes the decision. | This is usually the mother or the father. |

| ROLES | FAMILY MEMBERS |
|---|---|
| The *purchaser* purchases the products. | It is usually the mother's responsibility to purchase the groceries. |
| The *user* is the person who actually uses the product. | The baby consumes the vegetable purée purchased by the mother. |

Source: Adapted from McDaniel, C. and Darden, WR. 1987. *Marketing*. Boston: Allyn & Bacon, p 146.

### 4.3.2.3   Reference groups

Individuals may belong to many sorts of groups. A group consists of two or more people who interact with each other to accomplish some goal. Examples include families, close personal friends, co-workers, members of an organisation, leisure and hobby groups, and neighbours. Any of these groups may become reference groups.

*A reference group involves one or more people that a consumer uses as a basis for comparison or 'point of reference' in forming responses and performing behaviours*[18].   In all reference groups, there are distinctive norms of behaviour and members are expected to conform to these norms in order to avoid sanctions being applied against them.

The following types of reference groups influence consumer behaviour patterns:

- *Membership groups* are groups to which the person has obtained membership, for example friends or a social club.
- *Automatic groups* are groups to which a person belongs as a result of age, sex or occupation. A peer group is an example of an automatic group.
- *Negative groups* are groups with which a person does not wish to be associated. A person intentionally avoids the norms of the negative group; examples are smokers or drinkers.
- *Associative groups* are those groups to which a person aspires to belong, for example a group with higher status or level of acceptance amongst peers, or a celebrity or sports star.

Typical members of associative reference groups are often used as models in advertisements in order to show potential consumers the type of person who buys the product and also the way in which the product can be used.

The advertising message attempts to persuade potential customers to follow the example set by these models. Members of perceived negative groups can also be used in advertising; for example, overweight models in health food advertisements.

Reference groups affect consumer behaviour in three ways:

- **Normative influence** – norms of behaviour are laid down by the reference group and group members behave accordingly (they wear the same type/brand of clothes or shop at the same retail store).

- **Value – expressive influence** – behaviour portrays certain values, for example, health consciousness, environmental consciousness or ethical behaviour.

- **Informational influence** – consumers often accept the opinions of group members as credible, especially when it is difficult to assess product or brand characteristics by observation[19].

Reference group influence can extend to the decision to purchase a product as well as the choice of a specific brand. Bearden and Etzel[20] indicate the following situations where strong reference group influence occurs:

- **Publicly consumed luxuries** – strong influence on decision to buy product and the choice of the brand (for example, cellular phones).

- **Privately consumed luxuries** – strong influence on decision to buy product but not on brand (for example, water purifiers).

- **Publicly consumed necessities** – strong influence on brand choice (for example, a wrist watch).

- **Privately consumed necessities** – no reference group influence (for example, underwear or mattresses).

### 4.3.2.4  Opinion leaders

The opinion leader has an important function in the marketing communication process, acting as a go-between in what is known as the two-step flow of communication. Research results have indicated that information does not flow directly from the mass media to individual consumers in the target market but is channelled through a person, the **opinion leader**, who interprets and evaluates the information, relaying acceptance or rejection of the message to other consumers in the target market.

The role of the opinion leader is especially important in purchasing high-risk new products. In the case of a new fashion, for example, the fashion opinion leader is willing to accept the risk of ridicule or financial loss, which the ordinary consumer is usually anxious to avoid. The latter will only become interested after the new fashion has been vetted and approved by the opinion leader. This process of gradual acceptance is known as **diffusion**.

There is a great deal of overlap between leader and follower roles. Every consumer is a member of several different reference groups and is influenced by these groups as well as by the opinion leaders in these groups. In the same way, one person can be an opinion leader in one group while being a follower in another. The marketer must identify the relevant reference groups and the opinion leaders as this will ensure the effective communication of the advertising message and the acceptance of this message by the target market[21].

## 4.4 THE BUYING DECISION-MAKING PROCESS

When buying products, consumers follow a decision-making process shown in Figure 4.8. Not all consumers proceed in order through all the steps. Consumers engaged in extensive decision making go through all the steps. Each of the steps in the decision-making process will be discussed briefly.

### FIGURE 4.8  STAGES OF THE PURCHASE DECISION PROCESS

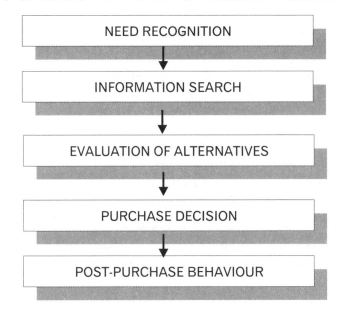

NEED RECOGNITION

INFORMATION SEARCH

EVALUATION OF ALTERNATIVES

PURCHASE DECISION

POST-PURCHASE BEHAVIOUR

## 4.4.1 Need recognition

The process by which a consumer makes a purchase decision begins when the consumer recognises a need. This phase is sometimes called the **problem recognition** or **problem awareness** phase. When an individual perceives a difference between the desired state of affairs and the actual state of affairs, an unsatisfied need is felt or recognised. A problem exists which must be dealt with as soon as possible. The recognition may come from an internal stimulus such as hunger, fatigue, or a desire to impress people. Alternatively, it may come from external stimuli such as an advertisement, the launch of a new product or an invitation to a party.

Marketing managers can, without any doubt, make consumers aware of unsatisfied or even dormant needs. It must be emphasised, however, that marketing messages cannot convince a person of unfelt needs. Marketing messages cannot persuade a consumer against his or her will.

Other reasons for consumers becoming aware of a need that can be satisfied by buying a specific product are as follows:

- the availability on the market of a new, improved product;
- a change in the consumer's circumstances (for example, more or less money available to spend);
- out-of-stock situations (a person buying groceries once a month); and
- dissatisfaction with the product currently in use.

## 4.4.2 Information search

After consumers have identified a need, they may then look for information about how best to satisfy that need. Whether the consumer does or does not search for more information depends on the perceived benefits of the search versus the perceived costs. The perceived benefits include finding the best price, obtaining the most desired model and achieving ultimate satisfaction with the purchase decision. The perceived costs include the time and expenses of undertaking the search. Consumers will spend time and effort searching as long as the benefits of the search outweighs the costs[22].

Depending on how much experience a consumer has in meeting a particular type of need, the consumer will seek information from the following sources[23]:

- *Internal sources*: There is information lodged in the person's memory. For routine purchases or those made out of habit (for example, shampoo), this may be the only source of information.

- *Group sources*: The consumer often consults with other people (family, friends and colleagues). These sources of information may be the most powerful in shaping purchase decisions, especially where the consumer is inexperienced or uncertain.

- *Marketing sources*: Consumers obtain information from marketers, through salespeople, advertisements, product displays and packages.

- *Public sources*: These are sources, independent of the marketer, for example, reports in the media or ratings by independent organisations or individuals.

- *Experiential sources*: The consumer may also experience the product while shopping, for example by handling it, tasting it, smelling it or trying it out.

From all these sources the consumer usually identifies several alternatives to satisfy the need. The set of alternatives that the consumer identifies is known as the **consideration set or evoked set**. The products or brands in the evoked set are the products or brands that the buyer can further evaluate. For example, there are more than 100 types of motorcars available, yet many consumers consider only four or five different types.

The extent to which an individual conducts an external search depends on the following factors:

- *Perceived risk* – the higher the risk the more extensive the search.

- *Knowledge level of the buyer* – the better informed the consumers are, the less they need to search for information.

- *Prior experience* – buyers with no prior experience in buying a certain product will spend more time seeking information.

- *Level of interest in the product* – a consumer who is more interested in a product will spend more time searching for information[24].

### 4.4.3  Evaluation of alternatives

Evaluation entails the appraisal by the consumer of the attributes and benefits of various alternatives. A host of criteria may be used to evaluate products.

The abundance of evaluation criteria involved in any major decision makes evaluation very difficult indeed. The decision maker must also decide on the relative importance of often conflicting criteria. In Figure 4.9 some product and psychological criteria which can be applied in the evaluation of alternatives are given.

## FIGURE 4.9 EVALUATION CRITERIA

| PRODUCT CRITERIA | PSYCHOLOGICAL CRITERIA |
|---|---|
| Cost/price | Satisfaction of social needs |
| Quality/durability | Satisfaction of ego needs |
| Aesthetic qualities (for example, colour, style and texture) | Image of product (or store) |
| | Contribution of the product to lifestyle |

Source: Van der Walt, *et al*. 1996. *Marketing management*. Cape Town: Juta, p 90.

Some of the criteria in Figure 4.9 can be evaluated in an objective way. Price, quality and performance standards of alternatives can be compared objectively, but personal and subjective factors play an important role in the evaluation of aesthetic qualities, the image of the product and the contribution of the chosen item toward need satisfaction and lifestyle. In the evaluation of alternative points of purchase (stores), the evaluation criteria may include the product assortment, hygiene considerations, the image projected by the store, and the conduct of the sales personnel.

Evaluation takes place in the mind of the consumer and is an example of covert behaviour. One cannot actually see someone weighing the alternative attributes of various products and those which have led to the final decision. Consumers are often unwilling to acknowledge that psychological criteria play an important role during the evaluation phase.

The perceived risks associated with buying a specific product also impact on the evaluation process. Figure 4.10 shows which risks are critically evaluated by a consumer during evaluation.

From Figure 4.10 it can be deduced, for example, that older people with a low income, experiencing ill health and suffering from anxiety caused by loss of self-esteem, status and affiliation with others, will probably be sensitive to most risk factors. It will be difficult for them to make a decision to purchase.

## FIGURE 4.10  RISK FACTORS CONSIDERED DURING EVALUATION

| TYPE OF RISK | TYPICAL CONSUMER | TYPE OF PRODUCT |
|---|---|---|
| Financial risk | Consumers with inadequate funds, with a low income or those sensitive to financial loss. | Expensive products, for example, homes and motocars. |
| Functional risk | Practical people for whom the functional aspects of products are deemed important. | Appliances requiring a degree of dedication, for example, computers and microwave ovens. |
| Physical risk | Older and disadvantaged people and those for whom health and vitality have high priority. | Mechanical products which can cause injuries, for example, health products and medicine. |
| Social risk | Individuals aiming to prove themselves and those that lack self-confidence. | Symbolic products, for example, fashion clothing, jewellery, sporting equipment and deodorants. |
| Psychological risk | Individuals who have a strong need for respect and status. | Expensive personal luxuries. |

Source: Solomon, MR. 1994. *Consumer behaviour*. Boston: Allyn & Bacon, p 228.

### 4.4.4 Purchase decision

After searching and evaluating, the consumer must decide whether to buy or not. If the decision is to buy, a series of related decisions must be made for example:

- brand decision;
- vendor decision;
- quantity decision;
- time decision; and
- payment method decision.

Figure 4.11 contains a summary of these decisions.

## FIGURE 4.11  WHERE, HOW MUCH, WHEN AND HOW CONSUMERS PURCHASE

### CONSUMER DECISION MAKING

| WHERE? | HOW MUCH? | WHEN? | HOW? |
|---|---|---|---|
| Supermarket | Purchases regularly | Time of day | Cash |
| Discount store | Purchase now and then | Day of the week | On credit |
| Department Store | Purchases never | Season | Lay-bye |
| Shopping centre | | | Hire purchase |

Source: Van der Walt, *et al*. 1996. *Marketing management*. Cape Town: Juta, p 99

## 4.4.5 Post-purchase behaviour

After purchasing the product, the consumer will experience some level of satisfaction or dissatisfaction. The marketer's job does not end when the product is bought, but continues into the post-purchase period.

Marketers must monitor post-purchase satisfaction, post-purchase actions and cognitive dissonance.

■ *Post-purchase satisfaction*[25]

What determines whether the buyer will be highly satisfied, somewhat satisfied, or dissatisfied with a purchase? The buyer's satisfaction is a function of the closeness between the buyer's product expectations and the product's perceived performance. If the product's performance falls short of customer expectations, the customer is disappointed; if it meets expectations, the customer is satisfied; if it exceeds expectations, the customer is delighted. These feelings make a difference in whether the customer buys the product again and discusses the product favourably or unfavourably.

Consumers form their expectations on the basis of messages received from sellers, friends and other information sources. If the seller exaggerates the benefits, consumers will experience unfulfilled expectations, which leads to dissatisfaction. The larger the gap between expectations and performance, the greater the consumer's dissatisfaction. Here the consumer's coping style comes into play. Some consumers magnify the gap when the product is not perfect and they are highly dissatisfied. Other consumers minimise the gap and are less dissatisfied.

■ *Post-purchase actions*

The consumer's satisfaction or dissatisfaction will influence future behaviour. A satisfied consumer will purchase the product again and spread positive messages about the product. Dissatisfied consumers will respond differently. They may stop using the product, may return the product or they may take some form of public action.

■ *Cognitive dissonance*

In making a final choice, the consumer had to forego other attractive options, and also had to part with (perhaps a great deal of) money, which could have been used for other purposes. It is no wonder, therefore, that the consumer often develops doubts regarding the wisdom of the decision. This negative feeling of doubt and uncertainty in the post-purchase period is referred to as *cognitive dissonance*[26], a negative emotion stemming from a psychological inconsistency in the cognitions (the things that a person knows).

Dissonant consumers will try to correct these psychological inconsistencies by attempting to convince themselves that the original decision was correct and very judicious. In order to do so, they may rationalise by putting forward logical reasons for decisions taken and may also turn to others for approval and reassurance.

The post-purchase evaluation phase can be regarded as the beginning of a new decision-making process. Will the consumer consider repurchasing the same product? Routine decision making develops when a brand loyal consumer insists on purchasing the same brand every time.

## 4.5 BUSINESS BUYING BEHAVIOUR

Businesses buy goods and services for the following purposes:

■ To manufacture other goods and services (for example, raw material, equipment, components and tools).

■ To resell to other organisational buyers or to consumers (for example, retailers or wholesalers).

■ To conduct the organisation's operations (for example, office equipment, stationery and cleaning materials [27]).

These products are bought according to planned and structured purchasing procedures by trained and well-informed buyers employed by the organisations. The buyer is not only knowledgeable about the enterprise's requirements but has also consulted and analysed outside sources of information. The buying decision is usually taken by more than just one person and is based on rational considerations. This is in contrast with consumer decisions, which are often based on the satisfaction of psychological and social needs.

The following issues regarding organisational buying behaviour will be discussed in paragraph 4.5.1:

■ How the behaviour differs from the consumer buying behaviour.

■ The buying decisions that buyers make.

■ The participants in the buying process.

■ How industrial buyers make their buying decisions.

## 4.5.1 Differences between organisational buying behaviour and consumer buying behaviour

The following are the unique characteristics of business buying behaviour:

■ There are usually more people involved in the purchasing process, each with a specific role to play.

■ The process is often technically more complex.

■ Buyers acquire products for further production, use in operations, or resale to final customers.

■ The purchase process tends to focus more on rational needs.

■ The post-purchase process is often more significant, for example, the need for service and installation.

■ There is a greater interdependency between buyer and seller as long-term relationships evolve.

■ Buyers are more likely to have unique needs that require customised manufacturing to specifications.

■ More personal selling is involved as both parties hammer out the details.

- Decisions are often more time-consuming (products are complex and a greater number of individuals are involved).

- Buyers must follow policies and compare guidelines which place restrictions on what and from whom they can buy.

### 4.5.2  Types of buying decisions[28]

The organisational buyer faces a set of decisions in making a purchase. The number and nature of the decisions depend on the buying situation. Four types of buying decisions can be distinguished:

- *New-task buying*. This is the most difficult and complex buying situation because it is a first-time purchase of a major product, for example, a computer system, production machinery or custom-built offices. Typically, several people are involved in the buying decision because the risk is great.

  Information needs are high and the evaluation of alternatives is difficult because the decision makers have little experience with the product. Marketers have the challenge of finding out what the buyers needs are and to communicate the product's ability to satisfy these needs.

- *Straight rebuy*. This is a routine, low-involvement purchase with minimal information needs and no great consideration of alternatives. It is usually handled by the purchasing department, who simply chooses from approved suppliers on its list. Suppliers who are not on this list may have difficulty with initial contact with the buyer. Examples are the repeat purchase of office supplies, chemicals, small components and bolts and nuts.

- *Modified rebuy*. This buying situation is somewhere between the other two in terms of time and number of people involved, information needed and alternatives considered. In a modified rebuy, the buyer wants to modify product specifications, prices, terms or suppliers and needs to evaluate suppliers on a regular basis. Examples are buying a new truck, personal computers, consulting services or components.

- *Systems buying*. Some buyers prefer to buy a packaged solution to a problem from a single supplier. This practice began with governments buying major weapons and communication systems. Instead of buying components and assembling the machinery, buyers ask for bids from suppliers who would supply the components and assemble the package or system.

Spoornet, for example, strives to produce a package of logistic services (transport, warehousing, insurance and shipment) to their key clients.

### 4.5.3 Buying centre

The decision-making unit of a buying organisation is called its *buying centre*. A buying centre can be defined as all the individuals and units that participate in the decision-making process. The size and make-up of the buying centre will vary for different purchases and for different buying situations. The individuals also differ in terms of their authority, the status of their positions, their credibility, and their degree of empathy.

The members of the buying centre can play any of the following roles:

- *Users* of the product or service. This category includes those people who usually initiate the act of purchasing and play an important role in defining the various purchasing specifications. Users can influence buyers' actions negatively (by, for example, refusing to use a particular supplier's product) or positively (by, for example, using a new product that is more cost-effective).

- *Influencers* are all people who have a direct or indirect influence on the purchasing decision, for example, engineers involved in the design of product specifications or the evaluation of alternatives.

- *Buyers* who have the authority to select suppliers and sign contracts.

- *Decision makers* concerned with the approval of transactions. In the case of routine purchases, the buyer usually makes the decision, but in the case of unique and important purchases, senior management usually approves the transaction.

- *Gatekeepers* are those individuals in the business who control the flow of information from one person/department to another person/department, for example, the restricting of salespeople from making direct contact with users or influencers.

In analysing the buying centre, a marketer strives to answer the following questions.

- Who are the individuals that form the buying centre?
- What is each member's power base?
- What is each member's relative influence in the decision?
- What are each member's evaluation criteria and how does he/she rate each prospective supplier on these criteria?

©Juta

## 4.5.4 Buying decisions

The organisation buying process consists of the following eight stages:

- **Problem recognition** – recognise a problem or need;
- **General need recognition** – describe general characteristics and quantity of needed item;
- **Product specification** – specify the best technical product specifications;
- **Supplier search** – try to find the best supplier.
- **Proposal solicitation** – invite qualified suppliers to submit proposals;
- **Supplier selection** – review proposals and select a supplier;
- **Order routine specification** – write final order, list technical specifications, quantity needed, delivery time, return policies, warranties and so on.
- **Performance review** – rate satisfaction with supplier, decide whether to continue, modify or stop using suppliers.

Buyers facing a new-task buying situation would probably go through all the stages of the buying process. Buyers making modified or straight rebuys will usually skip some of the stages in the buying process. See Table 4.3 for an indication of the steps in each buying situation.

## TABLE 4.3  Influence of buying situations on buying decisions

| BUYING STAGES | BUYING SITUATIONS | | |
|---|---|---|---|
| | New buy | Modified rebuy | Straight rebuy |
| Problem recognition | Yes | Maybe | No |
| General need recognition | Yes | Maybe | No |
| Production specification | Yes | Yes | Yes |
| Supplier search | Yes | Maybe | No |
| Proposal solicitation | Yes | Maybe | No |
| Supplier selection | Yes | Maybe | No |
| Order routine specification | Yes | Maybe | No |
| Performance review | Yes | Yes | Yes |

## SUMMARY

In this chapter, the focus is firstly on the individual consumer and the factors influencing consumer behaviour. Individual as well as group determinants influencing the decision-making process are described.

The chapter concludes with an overview of organisational buying behaviour. It describes the different decisions that buyers make, the participants in the decision-making process and the buying decisions.

In the next chapter, the emphasis falls on the various segments in the market. Marketing management direct its marketing offering to chosen segment(s) as it is improbable that all needs can be satisfied with a single market offering.

# REFERENCES

1. Adcock, D; Bradfield, R; Halborg, A and Ross, C. 1988. *Marketing principles and practice*. London: Pitman, p 61.

2. Kotler, P and Armstrong, G. 1994. *Principles of marketing*. Englewood Cliffs, NJ: Prentice Hall, p 171.

3. Assael, H. 1992. *Consumer behaviour and marketing action*. Boston: Kent, p 16.

4. Kotler and Armstrong pp 190 – 192.

5. Stanton, WJ; Etzel, MJ and Walker, BJ 1994. *Fundamentals of marketing*. New York: McGraw Hill, pp 166 – 167.

6. Stanton *et al* p 167.

7. Stanton *et al* p 168.

8. Wilkie, WL; 1994. *Consumer behaviour*. New York: John Wiley & Sons, p 216.

9. Wilkie p 257.

10. Boyd, HW; Walker, OC and Larreche, J. 1995. *Marketing management*. Boston: Irwin, p 125.

11. Lamb, CW; Hair, JF and McDaniel, C. 1996. *Marketing*. Cincinatti: South Western College Publishing, p 133.

12. Stanton *et al* p 173.

13. Lamb *et al* pp 133 – 134.

14. Engel, JF; Blackwell, RD and Mincard, PW. 1995. *Consumer behaviour*. New York: The Dryden Press, pp 433 – 434.

15. Van der Walt, A; Strydom, JW; Marx, S and Jooste, CJ. 1996. *Marketing management*. Cape Town: Juta, pp 83 – 84.

16. Van der Walt *et al* p 84.

17. Van der Walt *et al* pp 85 – 86.

18. Peter, JP and Olson, JC. 1994. *Understanding consumer behaviour*. Boston: Irwin, p 385.

19. Engel *et al* pp 719 – 725.

20. Bearden, WO and Etzel, MJ. 1982. *Reference group influence on product and brand purchase decisions*. Journal of Consumer Research. September, p 185.

21. Van der Walt *et al* pp 87 – 88.

22. Lamb *et al* p 116.

23. Churchill, GA and Peter, JP. 1995. *Marketing: creating value for customers*. Boston: Irwin, pp 249 – 250.

24. Lamb *et al* pp 116 – 117.

25. Kotler and Armstrong pp 197 – 199.

26. Peter and Olson p 168.

27. Stanton *et al* p 182.

28. Kotler and Armstrong pp 191 – 192 and Stanton *et al* p 195.

# CHAPTER 5

## MARKET SEGMENTATION, TARGETING AND POSITIONING

## 5.1 INTRODUCTION

The marketing concept states, amongst others, that the market offering must be focused on satisfying customer needs, demands and preferences optimally. In an ideal situation, the marketer would therefore respond with a custom-made product, a separate price, and an unique promotion and distribution strategy for every potential customer in the market. However, such a strategy would be far too expensive and demanding to execute in practice, especially in a heterogeneous market.

The question that might therefore arise is whether the marketing concept has any practical value. Is it a philosophy – a pipe dream – or is it merely a statement that serves to appease the critics of marketing?

The answer to these questions is an unequivocal 'No'! Because marketers were quick to realise that satisfying individual customer needs is far too costly and unrealistic, they decided to generalise about the needs, demands and preferences of the heterogeneous market. At the same time, marketers realise that they cannot be all things to all people – they must focus on satisfying specific customer needs and concentrate on what they do best to remain competitive in an increasingly competitive marketplace. How this can be achieved is the central theme of this chapter.

---

### LEARNING OUTCOMES

At the end of this chapter you will be able to:

- explain the concept of market segmentation;
- indicate how marketers can segment their market;

---

- highlight the prerequisites for effective market segmentation;
- explain what is meant by the term 'target marketing';
- suggest factors that should be considered when selecting a target market;
- explain the concept of product positioning;
- discuss the positioning process; and
- describe the positioning methods that marketers can pursue in practice.

## 5.2  SEGMENTATION, TARGETING AND POSITIONING DEFINED

To ensure its continuity and growth, an enterprise is dependent on, *inter alia*, the consumer and the satisfaction of his/her needs. Although the satisfaction of customer needs is not a goal in itself, it enables the enterprise to achieve its own goals. Therefore, the greater the need satisfaction customers can derive from an enterprise's products, the easier it becomes for the enterprise to achieve its own goals. To achieve maximum customer satisfaction, marketers therefore divide the heterogeneous market into fairly homogeneous subsets of customers. This process is referred to as **market segmentation**. Each segment of the market, it is assumed, will have similar needs, and will respond in a similar way to the market offering and strategy. The market for hotels can, *inter alia*, be subdivided into the following subsegments: business travellers, sports participants, conference delegates, holiday tourists, local travellers, overseas travellers, and so on. Each of these segments exhibits different characteristics and needs with regard to accommodation, facilities and services required. It follows that no single hotel can cater for all the unique needs of all these market segments.

The organisation must decide next which market segment(s) needs it can best satisfy. The Protea Hof hotel in Pretoria, which is situated in the city centre, has, for example, decided to cater primarily for the needs of the business traveller, and has therefore developed its product offering around the needs of business travellers. The process of deciding which segment(s) to pursue is referred to as **market targeting**.

Once the target market segment has been chosen, the enterprise must decide how to compete effectively in this target market. A decision has to be made concerning the competitive advantage to be achieved. This is known as *positioning*. The Protea Hof hotel can decide to compete on the basis of a lower price (when compared to competitors), or to compete on the basis of ambience and prestige, which would be reflected by the quality of the interior of the hotel, the professional service of its employees, and the availability of facilities and services required by business travellers, such as telefax machines, photocopy machines, secretarial services and chauffeurs. Alternatively, they may decide to compete on the basis of their superior location and accessibility to most government departments situated in Pretoria. The discussion in this chapter centres on these core concepts.

## 5.3   SEGMENTING THE MARKET

In this section, we deal with the following issues with regard to market segmentation: firstly, the merits and drawbacks of market segmentation are discussed; secondly, we turn our attention to the prerequisites of effective market segmentation. A discussion of the common bases used to segment consumer and industrial markets concludes this section.

### 5.3.1  Merits and drawbacks of market segmentation

Market segmentation offers the following benefits to marketers:

- Firstly, it forces marketers to focus more on customer needs. In a segmented market, the marketer can fully appreciate the differences in customer needs, and respond accordingly. A greater degree of customer satisfaction can be achieved if the market offering is developed around customer needs, demands and preferences.

- Secondly, segmentation leads to the identification of excellent new marketing opportunities if research reveals an unexplored segment. Without proper segmentation, such a market segment may remain untapped for years.

- Thirdly, market segmentation provides guidelines for the development of separate market offerings and strategies for the various market segments.

- Lastly, segmentation can help guide the proper allocation of marketing resources.

A large, growing market segment may be allocated a greater proportion of the marketing budget, while a shrinking one may be scaled down or eventually abandoned if it becomes unattractive.

However, market segmentation also has the following disadvantages which must be considered by the marketer:

■ The development and marketing of separate models and market offerings is very expensive. One standardised model is much cheaper to manufacture and to market.

■ Only limited market coverage is achieved, since marketing strategies would be directed at specific market segments only.

■ Excessive differentiation of the basic product may eventually lead to a proliferation of models and variations and finally cannibalisation. *Cannibalisation* occurs when one product takes away market share from another product developed by the same enterprise.

## 5.3.2   Prerequisites for market segmentation

Basically, market segmentation must enhance customer satisfaction and profitability of shareholders. To subdivide the market for small delivery vehicles into Western Cape and Natal farmers would make little marketing or business sense. In this case, geographic location makes no difference since the requirements of the farmers remain the same regardless of location. Geographic location would be very effective as a means of segmenting the market for insecticides, since farmers in the Western Cape have to deal with different insects to the farmers in KwaZulu-Natal. For market segmentation to be effective, it must meet the following criteria:

■ *It must be measurable*. The size, purchasing power, potential profit and profile of the segment must be measurable. If this is not possible, it would be extremely difficult to compare such a segment with others, or to properly assess its attractiveness.

■ *It must be large enough*. Pursuing a market segment that is too small is not profitable. A segment must be the largest homogeneous group of people worth exploiting with a tailored market offering and marketing strategy. Although South Africa boasts a large variety of cultures, some of them, such as the Chinese community, may be so small that it does not warrant special attention by marketers.

■ *It must be accessible*. The marketer must be able to reach the market segment with his/her market offering and strategy. How is it possible, for example, to reach rural people if they cannot read or do not listen to the radio? Such a segment is largely inaccessible to the marketer.

- **It must be actionable**: It must be possible to develop separate market offerings for different market segments. Smaller enterprises are often unable to develop different market offerings or marketing strategies, even if they realise that there are distinct differences between various segments.

- **It must be differentiable**: Different market segments must exhibit heterogeneous needs. In other words, people in different segments must have different needs, demands and desires. People in the same segment, on the other hand, must exhibit similar characteristics and needs. The marketer should also be able to distinguish the segments from each other without too much difficulty[1].

Once marketing management is satisfied that a specific segment conforms to these conditions, it can be considered as a possible target market.

### 5.3.3 Bases for segmenting consumer markets

#### 5.3.3.1 Variables used in segmentation

The marketing manager can utilise different variables to segment a market. These variables can generally be classified according to *geographic*, *demographic*, *psychographic* and *behaviouristic* bases. Table 5.1 provides a detailed analysis of these classification bases.

Table 5.1 shows the bases for segmenting consumer markets in the first column, while the different variables that can be used for each are shown in the second column. In the following sections we offer a brief explanation of each approach.

### TABLE 5.1 Bases for segmenting consumer markets

| BASES | POSSIBLE VARIABLES |
|---|---|
| **1. GEOGRAPHIC** | |
| ■ Region | Gauteng, Durban-Pinetown, Cape Peninsula, KwaZulu-Natal, North West. |
| ■ Size of city or town | Under 10 000, 10 000 to 20 000, 20 000 to 25 000, over 25 000 inhabitants. |
| ■ Density | Urban, suburban, rural. |
| ■ Climate | Summer rainfall, winter rainfall, hot and humid, hot and dry. |

| BASES | POSSIBLE VARIABLES |
|---|---|
| **2. DEMOGRAPHIC** | |
| ■ Age | Under 7, 7 to 13, 14 to 19, 20 to 34, 35 to 49, 50 to 65, older than 65 years. |
| ■ Gender | Male, female. |
| ■ Family size | 1 and 2, 3 and 4, more than 4 members. |
| ■ Family life cycle | Young, married, without children; young married with children; older married couples with children; older married couples without children living in; singles. |
| ■ Income | Under R10 000, R10 000 to R 30 000, R30 001 to R45 000, R45 001 to R60 000, R60 001 to R75 000, more than R75 000 per annum. |
| ■ Occupation | Professional and technical, managerial, clerical, sales and related services, farmers, retired, students, housewives, unemployed. |
| ■ Religion | Protestant, Catholic, Muslim, Hindu. |
| ■ Race | White, Black, Coloured, Asian. |
| ■ Education | Std 8, matric, diploma, degree, post-graduate. |
| **3. PSYCHOGRAPHIC** | |
| ■ Lifestyle | Conservative, liberal. |
| ■ Personality | Gregarious, authoritarian, impulsive, ambitious. |
| ■ Social class | Upper class, middle class, lower class. |
| **4. BEHAVIOURISTIC** | |
| ■ Purchase occasion | Regular occasion, special occasion. |
| ■ Benefits sought | Economy, service, convenience, prestige, speed. |
| ■ User status | Non-user, ex-user, potential user, regular user. |
| ■ Usage rate | Heavy user, medium user, light user. |
| ■ Loyalty status | None, medium, strong, absolute. |
| ■ Readiness stage | Unaware, aware, informed, interested, desirous, intending to buy. |
| ■ Attitude towards product | Enthusiastic, positive, indifferent, negative, hostile. |

Source: Adapted from Kotler, P. 1997. *Marketing management: analysis, planning, implementation and control.* Englewood Cliffs, NJ: Prentice Hall, p 257.

The following three factors are important:

1. A mutual relationship may exist between some of these bases. It is possible, for example, that there is a strong relationship between income, occupation and education on the one hand, and between family size and geographic region on the other. In the tourism industry, for example, there is a strong relationship between income, occupation and education and the likelihood of travel.[2]

2. Needs seldom relate to one segment base only. A specific marketing strategy is unlikely to be directed only to people with an income of R15 000 to R20 000 per year. A better description of a particular market segment often utilises more than one segment base, for example unmarried men between 30 and 40 years of age with an income of more than R140 000 per year and living in the Gauteng area.

3. The market segmentation bases described in Table 5.1 are not complete. In the tourism industry, for example, marketers also use distance travelled, trip purpose, and buyer needs and benefits sought as segmentation bases. The number of possible segmentation bases are to a great extent determined by the creativity of the marketing manager.

### 5.3.3.2  Geographic segmentation

In segmenting a market geographically, the marketer divides the total market into different geographical areas, such as countries or regions. Variations such as the size of the city or town or population density may also be appropriate bases. The enterprise can then decide to target only one or a limited number of geographical areas. If customers in different areas exhibit diverse needs, these differences can be addressed at local level.

Until the late 1980s, population density was thought to be a good predictor of consumer behaviour and needs. With the advent of black taxi operators during the late 1980s and the beginning of the 1990s, this has become an increasingly poor predictor, since more and more rural black people travel to the major cities and metropolitan areas to do their shopping.

In a fairly small geographic area such as Johannesburg, marketers realise there are diverse markets, such as the central, southern, northern, western, and eastern areas of Johannesburg that can be treated as separate market segments with diverse needs. Many smaller entrepreneurs have decided to confine their marketing and operations to only one or two of these segments.

### 5.3.3.3 Demographic segmentation

Demographic segmentation is probably the most common base for segmenting consumer markets. This may be because of the relative ease with which the approach can be applied, or because consumer needs are often strongly associated with these variables[3].

Traditionally, companies in South Africa, with its diverse population groups and cultures (as explained in greater detail in a previous chapter), used race heavily as a basis for market segmentation. The majority of research reports or business plans published during the 1970s and 1980s distinguished between the needs of Blacks, Whites, Coloureds and Asian consumers. Increasingly, however, companies are moving away from this approach, making more use of other segmentation variables such as income, education, lifestyle, living standards, and so on.

In 1993, the South African Advertising Research Foundation (SAARF) published their first Living Standards Measure (LSM) report, explaining how they arrived at eight LSM categories, using thirteen variables such as degree of urbanisation and ownership of cars and major appliances instead of the outmoded category of race[4].

Since then the SAARF LSM has become the most widely used marketing research tool in South Africa. The most recent LSM classification divides the population into eight LSM groups, 8 (highest) to 1 (lowest). LSM-7 and LSM-8 are divided into Low and High respectively. In Table 5.2 we provide a brief description of three of the LSM groups. Included is the LSM group 1, the LSM group 5 and LSM 8 (high). The Internet contains more information on the LSM.

It should be noted that, even in the 1990s, culture and religion remain powerful segmentation bases, primarily because the different cultures and religions have vastly different traditions, beliefs, taboos and preferences which must be accommodated. Differences include the languages that people speak, the food that people eat, the clothes that people wear, the sport that people watch or participate in, to mention only a few.

## TABLE 5.2 Description of selected LSM groups

| LSM 1 –10,9% of adult population | LSM 5 –14,8% of adult population | LSM 8 (H) – 4,9% of adult population |
|---|---|---|
| **DEMOGRAPHICS** There is a significantly higher than average incidence of females and 50+ year-olds in SAARF LSM1. A third of this group has had no formal schooling at all, and just under a further third have no more than some primary school education, leaving a balance of 29% with (mostly incomplete) high school education. Literacy levels are below average. SAARF LSM1s reside in rural areas, sustained by an average monthly household income of R621. 39% claim to be unemployed. The majority prefers to speak Nguni, with Zulu slightly more frequent than Xhosa. | **DEMOGRAPHICS** This is the first group that lives more in urban areas (83%, one in three in Gauteng) than in rural areas. It is still predominantly composed of Blacks, with slightly more males than average, and a definite tilt towards the younger categories. Nearly two thirds (63%) have been to high school, and post-matric experience begins to appear in this group. There are slightly fewer children than average. Average household income is R1 449 per month. | **DEMOGRAPHICS** Whites are strongly dominant in this group (88%), the other three races appearing in this group in roughly equal proportions. It is the most metropolitan group (59%), the oldest (68% over 35), the wealthiest (household incomes at an average of R9 938 a month), and the best educated (86% have reached matric or better, with 18% having been to university). A quarter (24%) are in professional or technical jobs, with a further 23% in sales or clerical positions. Only 1% claim to be unemployed, and job mobility is at its highest (every year, 9% move to new employment). 84% employ domestic help. |

# TABLE 5.2  Description of selected LSM groups (continued)

| LSM 1 –10,9% of adult population | LSM 5 –14,8% of adult population | LSM 8 (H) – 4,9% of adult population |
|---|---|---|
| **RESIDENCE**<br>83% of this group live in a traditional hut which they own. Two-thirds of these huts have earthen floors. No SAARF LSM 1s have access to mains electricity or piped water on their plots (and hence there are no flush toilets). There is a very low incidence of maintenance on these homes.<br><br>**FINANCIAL SERVICES**<br>This group does not use formal sector financial services. Even the informal ones are limited to extremely low level stokvel attendance (0,2% in any one month) and very few funeral policies (0,4%).<br><br>**PRODUCTS**<br>This group is more likely than any other to use sorghum beer and buy flour. Given the lack of mains electricity, battery purchasing levels are also one of the highest. While most FMCG items occur at well below average levels, lack of conventional refrigeration means the number buying longlife and powdered full cream milk, infant formula and coffee creamers are close to - in some cases even above - the population average. Other foods in this category are regular soups, loose tea (though it lags well behind tea bag usage) and bottled cooldrinks. A few over - the - counter medicines are bought (laxatives) and used (cough remedies and headache tablets) at close to average frequencies. | **RESIDENCE**<br>Traditional huts have virtually disappeared in this group, but compound dwellers are at their most numerous (6%) and informal settlements and backyard dwellers are still above average (9% and 6% respectively). So too (though not numerous, at 2%) are hostel occupants. Most (87%) have electricity and 93% have water (though it is an outside supply more often than inside). Virtually everyone has a toilet, three quarters of them flushing, and kitchen sinks appear to substantial numbers for the first time (29%)<br><br>**FINANCIAL SERVICES**<br>Apart from increased incidence of savings accounts (28%) and ATM cards (18%) little use is made of formal sector facilities, although funeral insurance is held by 7%. Even stokvels are only attended by 3% of this group each month.<br><br>**PRODUCTS**<br>This is the first group in which virtually all the FMCG items listed are used or bought at average, or even above average levels. There are some exceptions; for example, sorghum beer is less popular, but table wine is becoming more popular. Battery purchasing is decreased by diminished need. | **RESIDENCE**<br>One in twenty people live in a townhouse - almost as many as in flats (8%); the latter figure in particular differs from SAARF LSM 8-L's 13%. Basic services are universal, and 35% have a pool, 84% are owner occupiers, and mortgages (bonds) are at their maximum incidence at 52%.<br><br>**FINANCIAL SERVICES**<br>Most financial products are at their most widespread in this group. This particularly applies to credit cards (60%) and petrol/garage cards (31%), both over three times higher than the SAARF LSM8-L levels. Consistent with high employment rates, 80% are covered by medical aid and 30% have medical insurance. A half have retirement policies, 63% have life insurance, and 60% endowment policies. In any one year, 14% invest in stocks and shares. Over half (53%) have some sort of short-term insurance.<br><br>**PRODUCTS**<br>Many usage and purchase penetrations are (naturally) at their highest in this SAARF LSM. Some, however, tail off towards this end of the spectrum, among them chewing gum, bottled cooldrink (although diet cool drinks increase), hand-held ice cream, polony, viennas, canned vegetables, coffee creamers and powdered milks of all kinds. Alcohol in general - and especially wine - shows a substantial increase over earlier SAARF LSMs, though cigarettes (33%) fall back slightly from the highs of the immediately preceding groups. |

## TABLE 5.2 Description of selected LSM groups (continued)

| LSM 1 –10,9% of adult population | LSM 5 –14,8% of adult population | LSM 8 (H) – 4,9% of adult population |
|---|---|---|
| **DURABLES**<br>Four out of five SAARF LSM 1s have a radio.in their home, but only 6% have access to a TV and 2% to a hi-fi or music centre. Ownership of other durable items is minimal.<br><br>**SHOPPING HABITS**<br>SAARF LSM 1s are predominantly bulk shoppers who buy at their local supermarkets in the rural environs, and at other neighbourhood outlets. They show the lowest incidence of fresh meat and fruit and vegetable purchasing - those that do buy do so predominantly from their local supermarket, though above average numbers (6%) get meat mainly from farm or roadside butcheries. Clothing and footwear buying is at its least frequent in this group, no item being bought by more than 6% of the group in any three month period.<br><br>**LIFESTYLE**<br>One in ten SAARF LSM 1s took a holiday in the last year - all within South Africa, and all stayed with relatives/friends. 12% enjoy tending their gardens, while 2% pin their hopes on lottery tickets. | **DURABLES**<br>72% of SAARF LSM 5s have television sets in the home, and 88% own a radio. In addition, half have a hi- fi or music centre. These items still outpace the growing number of electric stoves (doubled to 37% in this group), as do refrigerators (also doubled, to 54%). Apart from these goods, however, durables remain few and far between.<br><br>**SHOPPING HABITS**<br>For the first time, the major retail chains record a strong presence. Meat, fresh fruit, vegetables and toiletries are bought by average numbers, with clothing and footwear purchases also at average frequencies.<br><br>**LIFESTYLE**<br>In spite of their relatively greater affluence, the holidaying pattern of SAARF LSM 5s is essentially the same as seen in all preceding groups; one in ten, within South Africa, staying with friends and relatives. They are more likely than SAARF LSM 1-4 to decorate their homes internally, but other maintenance activities continue at rather low levels. One in ten-of this group exercise. Restaurants, take-aways and gyms are at about 2%, but lottery tickets/scratch cards attract 17%. | **DURABLES**<br>Money is generally no barrier to acquiring durables for this group, but a few items have yet to reach 50%, principally dishwashers (31%) and PCs (48%). (Individual washing machine types also fall into the sub-50% category, but as a group, their penetration is virtually 100%). Microwaves (96%), dishwashers (31%), tumble dryers (64%) and VCRs (90%) are all a significant step above SAARF LSM 8-L levels. One in three (32%) has a cellular phone.<br><br>**SHOPPING HABITS**<br>In line with greater family mobility and (probably) greater control over working patterns, two in five (the highest level of any SAARF LSM) buy their food and groceries in smaller, more frequent quantities. The use of Hypermarkets is greatest in this group. People in this group are, by a substantial margin, the most frequent buyers of all types of clothing and shoes.<br><br>**LIFESTYLE**<br>Most leisure activities record their highest levels in SAARF LSM 8-H. Air travel penetration reaches one in four (26% internal flight in 12 months; 25% flying to a foreign country every three years), and 68% take at least one annual holiday. Of the latter, nearly half are spent in time-share accommodation, with approximately a further third spent with friends or relatives. Though nearly 9% visit game park venues, the bulk (49%) visit coastal resorts. Home maintenance (R1 000) reaches 37% here, with 30% painting interiors, 22% exteriors, and 31% spending over R500 on DIY materials each year. Over a quarter (27%) have arrangements with domestic security firms. One in five (19%) is a member of a gym, and 40% take an active interest in gardening - these are both higher levels than in other SAARF LSMs. Exactly a third buy lottery tickets or scratch cards during the year. |

## TABLE 5.2 Description of selected LSM groups (continued)

| LSM 1 –10,9% of adult population | LSM 5 –14,8% of adult population | LSM 8 (H) – 4,9% of adult population |
|---|---|---|
| **MEDIA**<br>Fewer than half this group can be reached via the radio on any one day. Ukhozi FM and Radio Transkei achieve significantly high and above-average penetrations. Print media exposure is negligible. Outdoor Billboards (43% in the past 4 weeks) is the only other mass advertising medium available apart from radio. | **MEDIA**<br>SAARF LSM 5 is the first group where the numbers listening to the radio and watching TV on an average day are similar - 69% and 61% respectively. SABC 1 especially, but also SABC 2 are the TV channels of choice. On radio, although African ethnic stations predominate, Radio Metro attracts an above average 14%. Other English and Afrikaans stations do not feature, however. Print begins to play a larger role, with one in three reading a newspaper and a similar proportion reading a magazine, principally publications aimed at the non-white market. Cinema attendance in the last 12 weeks rises to 8%. | **MEDIA**<br>Again, there is a marginal increase in exposure to radio and TV (each 83%) in this group compared to preceding ones. Satellite dish penetration reaches 6%, with two thirds of these having access to DSTV, M-Net attracts 45% of the potential audience, and SABC 3 39% - well ahead of SABC 1 – 27% and SABC 2 – 29%. The most popular radio stations are 5FM and Jacaranda (both 14%) followed by Radio Sonder Grense (12%) and Highveld Stereo (10%). Wealth and education combine to provide print with its highest penetrations; magazines 81% and newspapers 73% combining at 96% for any print medium. |

Source: Adapted from SAARF. 1999. [Online]. Internet: http://saarf.co.za/lsm's.thm

### 5.3.3.4 Psychographic segmentation

Psychographic segmentation involves the segmentation of the market by means of categories such as social class, lifestyle or personality. To establish the different lifestyle categories, information concerning the respondents' attitudes, interests, and opinions (AIO) or values and lifestyles (VALS) is collected and then subjected to factor analysis to identify separate subgroups.

Locally, the AC Nielsen MRA Sociomonitor Value Groups survey is the most authoritative psychographic profile of its kind in South Africa. In order to create the Value Groups, respondents answer an extensive battery of psychographic statements. Their answers are then grouped and scored, giving every single respondent a different score and position on the 'social map', depending on their answers.

These scores are then statistically analysed and the Value Groups - broad groups of consumers with similar values, attitudes, and motivations (psychographics) – are established. The five Value Groups embrace the full spectrum of values among South African adults. They help marketers to understand what motivates their customers, and hence how best to appeal to them. The data can also aid marketers in more effective media placement.

Five Value Groups have been identified from the 1997 all adults database. These are the as follows:

1. Conformists (19,6% of all adults, or 5,042 million people).

2. Transitionals (20,5% of all adults, or 5,278 million people).

3. Progressives (18,8% of all adults, or 4,833 million people).

4. Non-Conformists (17,0% of all adults, or 4,375 million people).

5. Today-ers (24,1% of all adults, or 6,193 million people).

Table 5.3 contains a condensed profile of the five Value Groups, according to the latest Sociomonitor reports available from AC Nielsen MRA.

## TABLE 5.3 Sociomonitor value groups

**CONFORMISTS (19,6% of the adult population, or 5,042 million adults)**

This Value Group is characterised by conformity to group value systems. Traditions, religion and the family and home are paramount. Probably because of their civil and group-adhering values, they would like to see harmony between the different race groups, the South African nation as a whole, and the genders. They are accepting and understanding of others' emotions. Probably because of their strongly religious orientation, they are not comfortable with sexual liberty issues. They feel more secure within group norms than as individuals. They would rather be looked up to and accorded status for socially acceptable or civil behaviour, than for materialistic reasons. Familiarity makes them most comfortable; they do not usually desire too much novelty, excitement or risk. As a result of their adherance to traditions and the familiar, they are typically not comfortable with new products and technology and would probably need coaxing to change from the brands they use. Practicality comes before beauty – price and usefulness are the overriding factors in their purchase decisions.

## TABLE 5.3  Sociomonitor value groups (continued)

**TRANSITIONALS (20,5% of the adult population, or 5,278 million adults)**

This Value Group is characterised by traditional values with some focus on personal achievement and thus the assumption of individualistic and more modern values. The more traditional values are group-oriented, such as past-orientation, uBuntu, familism, religion, and cultural customs. Consequently, there is a strong group-orientation, but a stronger need for novelty and self-achievement, and not always automatic acceptance of all authority, rules and/or group-oriented conventions. They take pride in their own achievements and are materialistic – it is important that others see what they have achieved. Despite their status and materialistic orientation, price consciousness and practicality prevail over aesthetics in their purchase decisions. As part of their self-focus, health and their looks are also important. Unlike the Conformists, the Transitionals are not too outward-looking and are slightly hardened to others beyond their immediate circles – so despite their softer traditional values, they are not as accepting of other races or individual choices as what the Conformists are.

**PROGRESSIVES (18,8% of the adult population, or 4,833 million adults)**

The progressives are a modernised group whose primary needs are self-development but also some harmony in acquiring meaning from and giving back to the group. They are proudly focussed on self- improvement and development of every aspect of their personal lives – so they like to take care of, enhance, and project beautiful physical looks, their health, and home environments; and want to acquire new skills to stimulate their minds. Quality and intrinsics are a primary need in everything they do, including purchasing. There is some materialism and a desire to show others what they have achieved or acquired. They are comfortable with new technology, but do not need novelty or sensation for excitement. Probably as part of their search for meaning, there is acceptance that they are part of a bigger picture, and therefore some embracing of traditional and religious norms. However, not all traditions are automatically adhered to if they are not relevant to their lives (for example, they are below average in terms of familism, past-orientation and African customs). There's also empathy with others' feelings.

**NON-CONFORMISTS (17,0% of the adult population, or 4,375 million adults)**

This group rejects any group-oriented, civil, and/or traditional values in favour of individualism. They tolerate and accept other individuals easily, regardless of gender or race differences, and uphold one's rights to individual choice. Non-Conformists are drawn to technology and technological gadgetry – these are the people who take readily and comfortably to new technology. Nevertheless they are not materialistic for the sake of materialism, and shun the ownership of material goods merely to impress others. The goods that they acquire will be selected for their technological innovation and relevance to their lives. As part of their anti-establishment stance, they do not relate to conventional definitions of success and status. As individuals they have enough self-confidence to stand alone, so do not believe in making the effort to improve their looks or immediate surroundings, or furthering their education or skills, merely for the sake of it. They live their lives slightly on the edge – there is a tendency to want, or actually indulge in, raw thrills, fun and action rather than too much of the 'softer' self-development activities.

## TABLE 5.3  Sociomonitor value groups (continued)

**TODAY-ERS (24,1% of the adult population, or 6,193 million adults)**

Today-ers present a tough do not-care exterior to the world. There is a strong rejection of anything resembling group-civility or conventions. They are extrinsics-oriented – they will buy on brand externals and lower price rather than intrinsics, and need to show off to others what they have and who they are. There is an inclination for thrills and action, and living on the edge. Stimulants and relaxants like alcohol, cigarettes, maybe other drugs and sex too, are used for sensation and escapism. There is little acceptance or tolerance for the rights to individual sexual choice, or equality of the genders, and little feeling for or understanding of others, especially for those outside their relatively narrowly-defined sense of who and what is acceptable. For all their rough and tough attitude, Today-ers have little to look forward to and have little self-confidence as individuals. Hence the need for bolstering from their peer group. Despite being materially aspirational and extrinsics-bound, they take little interest in self-improvement of any form. This probably has a lot to do with lack of opportunities - consequently they feel disempowered and cannot relate to their personal part in improving their situation. This also means that they are generally out of touch with the latest technology or western developments (and they tend to live more in the past than in the future).

Source: Adapted from AC Nielsen MRA Sociomonitor 1997. 1999.

### 5.3.3.5  Behaviouristic segmentation

Buyers can also be segmented on the basis of their buying behaviour. This may take the form of the following:

■ *Purchase occasions*

Some buyers may use a product very regularly, whilst others may use it only on special occasions. Orange juice and champagne are two examples of products that fall into this category. Orange juice is often drunk mainly with breakfast, while champagne is mostly drunk on special occasions such as graduation, engagements and weddings. Consumption of these products can be increased by promoting the use of them at other occasions, such as lunches and dinners in the case of orange juice, or Valentine's day in the case of champagne.

■ *Benefits sought*

Some market segments may be very specific in what benefits they seek when buying a specific product. Some may seek economy in a computer printer, while others may prefer speed or after-sales support. When consumers are very specific with regard to the benefits they seek, marketers can respond with products that address these needs. In so doing, they satisfy their customers' needs.

■ *User status*

Consumers can be segmented into groups consisting of the non-users, ex-users, potential users or regular users. A balanced approach would require that an enterprise focus on both regular users as well as potential users. While the regular users guarantee survival in the short- to medium-term, potential users who can be enticed to become users, represent future growth.

■ *Usage rate*

Marketers can make provision for different market segments, based on how frequently buyers buy their products. Heavy users should receive special attention by marketers, since they may represent the bulk of sales revenue. It is therefore common to see hotels and airlines develop special clubs or frequent flier programmes to appeal to this important segment of the market.

■ *Loyalty status*

Consumers vary in the degree of loyalty they have towards the organisation or its brand names. On the one extreme, one finds the switchers, or those consumers who show no loyalty toward any brand. They can be attracted through frequent sales, but it may sometimes not be worthwhile attracting them. On the other hand, there are very loyal buyers. Hardcore loyals would insist on a particular brand, and would go to great lengths to acquire it. Ideally, they should be retained, and where possible they should be encouraged to become spokespeople for the organisations' products and services, as suggested by the relationship marketing philosophy.

■ *Buyer readiness stage*

Different marketing approaches have to be followed, depending on the consumer's readiness to buy. Potential consumers who are unaware of the product must first be made aware of it, while those who intend buying the product, must be convinced to do so. When cellular telephones were introduced to the South African market, most people were either unaware or aware (but not informed) about the product. Initially, awareness for the product had to be established. As awareness increased, more aggressive strategies were followed in the marketing of cellular telephones.

■ *Attitude towards the product*

By segmenting consumers according to their attitude towards the product, an enterprise can increase their marketing productivity.

Market segments that are negative or hostile towards a product can be avoided, saving valuable time and money. Attempts can be made to persuade those who are indifferent, while those who are enthusiastic or positive can merely be encouraged to support the product in future. Kotler (1997) quotes the political campaigner as an example in this regard. Hostile and negative voters are avoided, while the enthusiastic and positive ones are merely reminded to vote on election day. More time is spent with indifferent voters in order to persuade them to support a specific party.

## 5.3.4 Developing segment profiles

Every segment considered by the enterprise must be described fully with respect to its size, demographic and psychographic details, lifestyle, behaviour patterns and product usage. Such a profile enables marketing management to develop products that will provide the need satisfaction utilities desired by customers and to design marketing communication messages that will appeal to these customers. In a later section, we provide practical hints on how to accomplish this.

## 5.3.5 Bases for segmenting industrial markets

Traditionally, industrial firms were reluctant to accept marketing segmentation as a marketing tool[5]. This can be attributed to the fact that industrial firms tend to be more engineering-oriented, often focusing on product specifications rather than customer requirements. On the other extreme, one may find many industrial firms producing customised products or services to their customers. Consequently, they have no need to segment their market; they are producing for individual customers. Currently, the importance of market segmentation is increasingly realised by business-to-business marketers. Table 5.4 shows the most popular bases for segmenting industrial markets. It is clear that the marketer will consider totally different variables when segmenting the industrial market.

## TABLE 5.4 Bases for segmenting industrial markets

**DEMOGRAPHIC**
On which industries should we focus?
What size company must we target?
Number of employees in the organisation?
Which geographical areas must we target?
How long has the company been in business?
Does the company have one/multiple establishments?
Is it a local/national/international company?

## TABLE 5.4 Bases for segmenting industrial markets (continued)

**OPERATING VARIABLES**
On what technologies should we focus?
On what user types should we focus (heavy, medium, light, non-users)?
On what product types must we focus?
How frequently does the customer require delivery?
Should we focus on customers requiring many/few services?

**PURCHASING APPROACHES**
How centralised/decentralised is the purchasing function?
Should we focus on companies that seek quality/service/lower price?
Should we focus on companies that demand quick delivery/convenience/reputation/economy?
Should we focus on the companies with which we have strong links or should we target the most desirable ones?
Should we focus on those that prefer leasing/service contracts/systems purchases/sealed bidding?
Should we focus on organisations that are financial/marketing/production/engineering dominated?

**SITUATIONAL FACTORS**
Should we focus on customers who require quick and sudden delivery or should we focus on those that require steady delivery?
Should we focus on specialised application of our product or on all applications?
Should we be focusing on small/medium/large orders?

**PERSONAL CHARACTERISTICS**
Should we focus on companies who have similar values to ours?
Should we concentrate on risk takers or risk avoiders?
Should we focus on companies that show high loyalty towards their suppliers?

Source: Adapted from Assael, H. 1993. *Marketing: principles and strategy*. Fort Worth: Dryden Press, p 350.

In particular, the marketer can employ the following bases:

### ■ *Demographic dimensions*

Any demographic dimensions such as company size, as reflected in the sales volume, number of employees or other criteria; geographical area, number of outlets, or scope of operation (local/national/ international), can be used to classify companies into market segments.

### ■ *Operational variables*

Companies can also be classified according to their operational characteristics such as technology, user types, product types, or frequency of delivery.

■ *Purchasing approaches*

Marketers of industrial products often have to negotiate with the purchasing departments of other businesses. It would therefore make sense to segment the market along these dimensions. Among the most important variables to be used is the degree of centralisation/ decentralisation of the purchasing function, the power structure of the companies, the nature of the existing relationship with the customer, the purchasing criteria employed by the company, and so on. In a centralised purchasing department, for example, the buyer is more likely to consider all transactions with suppliers on a global basis, to emphasise cost savings, and to minimise risks. A decentralised purchasing department will, on the other hand, be more concerned with the user's need, will tend to emphasise product quality and prompt delivery and is likely to be less cost conscious[6].

■ *Situational factors*

Criteria such as the delivery requirements of customers, the product application, or the order size are regarded as situational factors. Often the marketer will find that about 80% of sales will be to customers who order in large quantities, while only about 20% will be to customers that buy in smaller quantities. The needs and demands of these segments will often vary greatly, justifying segmentation along these lines.

■ *Personal characteristics*

Marketers may also choose to segment the industrial market on the basis of the organisational values, risk profile or loyalty towards suppliers. Customers who are loyal to their suppliers can, for example, be treated with less aggression by salespeople, whilst the salesperson will have to be more aggressive in an attempt to retain the less loyal market segments. It is also advisable to spread one's risk between risk-takers and risk-avoiders, which decreases the likelihood of a disaster.

As in the case of the consumer market, the industrial marketer must compile a comprehensive description of the characteristics, needs and demands of the various market segments, based on the criteria provided in this section. Figure 5.1 provides guidelines in this regard.

Firstly, it is necessary to identify the various market segments in the particular market. The manager must then list the characteristics of each of these segments. Thirdly, the marketer would derive the needs and preferences of each segment by studying the characteristics of each segment. Once this has been done, the product or service can be developed around the needs of the identified market segment(s).

## FIGURE 5.1 COMPILING A PROFILE OF THE INDUSTRIAL MARKET

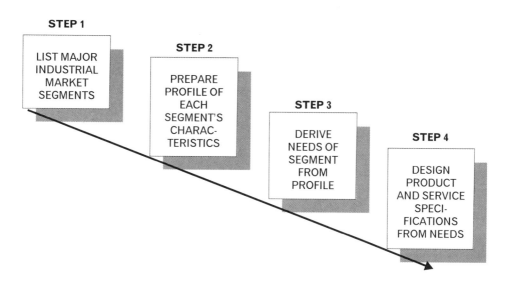

This process allows the marketing manager to adapt his/her marketing strategy to the unique requirements of the targeted market segments. In an increasingly competitive business environment, this can only enhance the competitiveness of the enterprise.

## 5.4 MARKET TARGETING

Once the marketer has developed a complete profile of the various segments in the market, he/she must to select one or more segments on which to concentrate the market offering.

This is known as *market targeting*. In this section, the focus is, firstly, on the criteria to be used to evaluate market segments, and, secondly, on the approaches available to the enterprise.

### 5.4.1 Selecting potential target markets

Before a specific market segment is selected as a target market it must first be evaluated according to five important evaluation criteria:

1. *Segment size and growth possibilities*

   A target market need not necessarily be big. A small segment can often be more profitable than one in which a large sales volume can be realised.

Marketing management must be convinced that there are further growth possibilities, thus making the segment sustainable. The so-called black tourism market may have been fairly small in size at the beginning of the 1990s, but its growth potential is immense, making it a very attractive segment for the new millennium.

2. **Attractiveness and potential profitability**

The attractiveness of a target market lies not only in its size and growth possibilities, but also in the promise of long-term profitability. Attractive segments attract competitors and intense competition can have a detrimental effect on future profits. Serious threats to attractive segments are aggressive competitors that can launch price wars or intensive advertising campaigns or competitors who are able to develop new substitute products. The growing power of buyers and suppliers also threatens attractive target markets. If the threat is very serious, an enterprise that does have the necessary resources and skills can decide not to take the opportunity to select the segment as a target market.

A target market is generally attractive if it has some degree of interrelationship with other segments. Instead of serving a number of small segments, it would be much better to combine interrelated segments. Interrelationships exist among segments that use the same raw materials, similar production methods or joint distribution channels.

3. **The resources and skills of the enterprise**

Promising segment opportunities that do not fit in with the long-term objectives set by management cannot be utilised. The same applies when resources and skills to exploit the opportunity are lacking. A segment can only be chosen as a target market if marketing management is fully committed to serving this target market better than any other competitor. This implies that the market offering must have an undoubted differential advantage to target market members. If not, it would be advisable to commit the cost and energy to an alternative option.

4. **Compatibility with the enterprise's objectives**

Apart from the resources and skills of the enterprise, the choice of a target must also consider the compatibility with the objectives of the enterprise. If it is found that the objectives of the enterprise cannot be enhanced by the choice of a particular market segment, it should be disregarded.

5. *Cost of reaching the target market*

When a potential target market is inaccessible to an enterprise's marketing strategies, or the cost to reach it is too high, it should not be considered[7].

## FIGURE 5.2  STEPS IN THE EVALUATION OF POTENTIAL MARKET SEGMENTS

Source: Adapted from Walker, OC; Boyd, HW and Larréché, JC. 1996. *Marketing strategy: planning and implementation*. Chicago: Richard D Irwin, p 162.

In order to assess the potential of each of the market segments identified during the segmentation process, Walker, Boyd and Larréché[8] propose five steps, shown in Figure 5.2. These steps are highlighted briefly in the following paragraphs.

The evaluation of potential market segments starts with the selection of a set of criteria which can be used to assess, firstly, the attractiveness of the particular target market and secondly, the competitive position of the enterprise with regard to a specific market segment. Because not all evaluation criteria are of equal importance, these factors are then weighed to reflect the relative importance of each.

The enterprise would then rate every market segment considered by the enterprise. Scores that reflect the market attractiveness and competitive position of the enterprise are then posted on a market attractiveness/ business position matrix. Such a matrix is shown in Figure 5.3. Once this has been done, the marketing manager will consider likely future changes that might manifest themselves. The arrow of Segment A in Figure 5.3 shows that this segment is expected to become less attractive in the future, while the organisation also believes that their competitive position will deteriorate. It is critically important to consider likely future changes, since the choice of a particular target market commits the enterprise to this market. Should changes occur in the future, the competitive position of the enterprise may be adversely affected.

## FIGURE 5.3   MARKET ATTRACTIVENESS/BUSINESS POSITION MATRIX

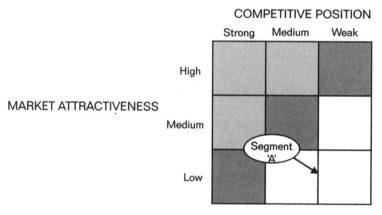

Source: Adapted from Walker, OC; Boyd, HW and Larréché, JC. 1996. *Marketing strategy: planning and implementation*. Chicago: Richard D Irwin, p 166.

Given these possible changes, the marketing manager will lastly evaluate the implications of possible future changes with regard to its impact on company strategies and resource requirements. Only once this has been completed will the marketing manager finally choose a market segment or segments to target.

## 5.4.2   Targeting market segments

Marketers may choose one, two or multiple market segments to target. In essence, marketers can choose between three broad segmentation approaches to the market: **concentrated targeting**, **differentiated targeting**, and **undifferentiated targeting**. Figure 5.4 reflects these approaches.

### ■ Concentrated targeting

Concentrating the market offering on one specific segment can lead to greater expertise in production, distribution and marketing communications. Because the product offering is aimed at one market segment only, it would be fair to argue that the enterprise will also be able to achieve greater customer satisfaction in this singular market segment. A big disadvantage, however, is that all efforts are then concentrated on one source. The risk of product failure and non-acceptance of the product is thus concentrated in a single target market. Should the preferences of the target market change, or should competitors enter the market with an improved offering, the enterprise may find itself without any business.

### ■ Differentiated targeting

In differentiated market segmentation, the enterprise elects to target two or more market segments, developing a unique marketing strategy for each one. This strategy allows the organisation to cater for the diverse needs of the different segments. It is, however, a costly strategy. In order to cater for the diverse needs, the enterprise incurs extra production costs as production runs become smaller, advertising costs increase because communication strategies must be adapted for the different market segments, administrative costs will increase as separate marketing plans have to be developed, and inventory costs increase as a greater variety of products must be maintained.

### ■ Undifferentiated marketing

When an undifferentiated marketing strategy is employed (also known as the **aggregation strategy**), the enterprise chooses to ignore the differences that are found in the market.

Instead, they pursue the total market with one basic market offering. In practice, the enterprise would concentrate on the commonalities of the market segment, rather than on the differences. One of the major advantages of such a strategy is the economies of scale that can be achieved with a standardised product and marketing strategy. This strategy has lost ground in recent years, as consumers have become more discriminating.

Refer to figure 5.4 for an illustration of concentrated targeting, differentiated targeting and undifferentiated marketing.

## FIGURE 5.4  APPROACHES TO MARKET TARGETING

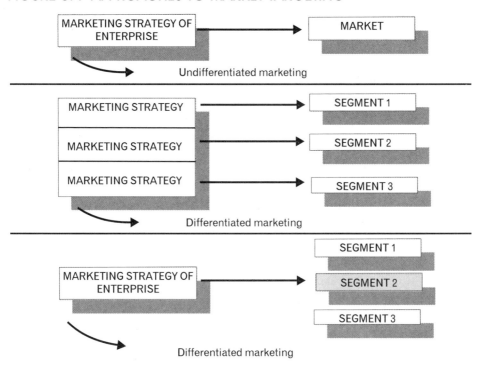

Source: Adapted from Kotler, P. 1994. *Marketing management: analysis, planning, implementation and control.* Englewood Cliffs, NJ: Prentice Hall, p 286.

# 5.5 PRODUCT POSITIONING

Product positioning refers to the way customers perceive a product in terms of its characteristics and advantages, and its competitive positioning. It therefore involves the creation, in the minds of the targeted buyers, of a distinctive position with regard to the organisation's product relative to the products of competing organisations. For positioning to be effective, it is important that the marketer understands customer buying criteria and recognises the performance of each competitor on each of the evaluative criteria.

## 5.5.1  Product positioning maps aid decision making

Marketers often use positioning or perceptual maps to portray market positions visually. A perceptual map is a multidimensional graphic image depicting consumer perceptions. These maps assist marketers in developing focussed marketing mixes or strategies. It also helps the manager to assess the advantage of an organisation's marketing program[9].

Figure 5.5 offers an example of a positioning map for South African luxury motor vehicles. The map shows how consumers perceive the various models. The closer a model lies to a particular variable, the more that model is associated with this variable. There are various gaps on the map, where no model is shown. Gaps like these are referred to as **competitive gaps**, and may indicate ideal marketing opportunities for the enterprise. However, marketers must proceed cautiously: these gaps may exist because it may be technically impossible to fulfill this requirement, or because it is an undesirable position due to limited customer interest.

## FIGURE 5.5 POSITIONING MAP FOR LUXURY VEHICLES IN SOUTH AFRICA

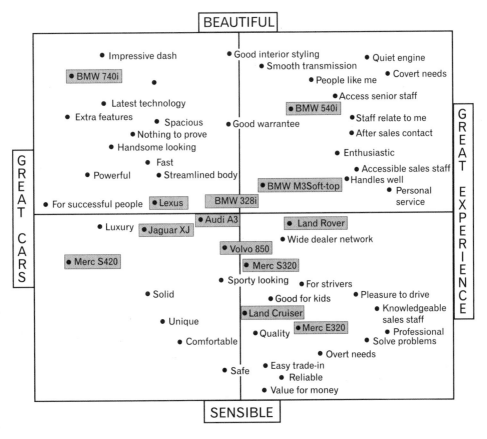

Source: Supplied by Toyota SA.

Many other variables or determinants, such as those listed later in this chapter, can be used to compile similar positioning maps. However, marketing information and sophisticated statistical testing is necessary for the development of positioning maps.

## 5.5.2 The positioning process

A seven-step approach can be adopted when positioning brands. (The term 'brands' is preferred here since it is individual producers' brands, not products, that compete against each other in a market. Positioning maps can, however, also be developed for product categories.) These steps are shown in Figure 5.6 and are discussed in this chapter.

## FIGURE 5.6 THE POSITIONING PROCESS

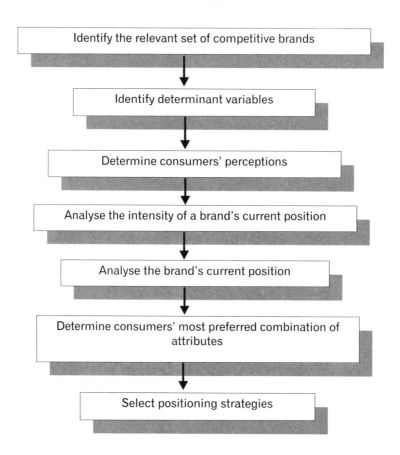

Source: Adapted from Walker, OC; Boyd, HW and Larréché, JC. 1996. *Marketing strategy: planning and implementation*. Chicago: Richard D Irwin, p 180.

## 5.5.2.1 Identify a relevant set of competitive brands

The positioning process starts with the identification of a relevant set of competitive brands to which a particular producer's brand will be compared. It is essential that all relevant competing brands must be identified in order to make the positioning effort worthwhile. This enables the marketer to identify the strengths and weaknesses of his/her own brand against a competing brand. It also helps him/her to decide whether to reposition the brand in order to strengthen its position in the market. **Repositioning** refers to the changing of a brand's (mostly undesirable) position in the market in the hope that the new positioning would improve the brand's appeal among consumers.

## 5.5.2.2 Identify relevant determinant or differentiation variables

In essence, product positioning has to do with competitive differentiation and the effective communication of this to customers. Kotler[10] suggests that an enterprise or market offering can be differentiated along four different dimensions: product, services, personnel or image. Table 5.5 summarises the main differentiation variables suggested by Kotler. These are not the only variables that can be used, but the most obvious ones have been discussed.

## TABLE 5.5  Differentiation variables

| PRODUCT | SERVICES | PERSONNEL | IMAGE |
|---|---|---|---|
| ■ Product features<br>■ Performance quality<br>■ Conformity to the target standard<br>■ Durability<br>■ Reliability<br>■ Repairability<br>■ Style<br>■ Design | ■ Delivery<br>■ Installation<br>■ Customer training<br>■ Consulting service<br>■ Repair<br>■ Miscellaneous | ■ Competence<br>■ Courtesy<br>■ Credibility<br>■ Reliability<br>■ Responsiveness<br>■ Communication | ■ Symbol<br>■ Media<br>■ Atmosphere<br>■ Events |

Source: Adapted from Kotler, P. 1997. *Marketing management: analysis, planning, implementation and control.* Englewood Cliffs, NJ: Prentice Hall, p 283

The marketer must decide which of the above (or other) differentiation variables should be used in developing a positioning map. In this case, Walker, Boyd and Larréché[11]  refer to **determinant variables**. They suggest that marketers must select those variables that play a major role in helping customers to differentiate among alternative brands in the market.

The following example serves to illustrate the importance of using determinant variables. Although safety is a major concern for all airline passengers, it is not regarded as a determinant variable as most customers use other features such as price, convenient flying times, service or frequent flier programmes to differentiate between competing airlines. Appropriate marketing research can aid the marketer in identifying determinant variables.

### 5.5.2.3  Determine consumers' perceptions

The marketer must establish how consumers perceive the various brands in terms of the determinant variables selected in the previous step. This step involves the collection of primary data from a sample of consumers. Using a structured questionnaire, these consumers (named respondents) are questioned about their perceptions of the various brands. The collected data is then analysed, using several statistical techniques. These include factor analysis, discriminant analysis, multidimensional scaling and so on.

### 5.5.2.4  Analyse the intensity of a brand's current position

When a consumer is unaware of a brand, such a brand cannot occupy a position in the mind of the consumer. In such instances, brand awareness must first be established. However, when a consumer is aware of a brand, the intensity of awareness may vary. In many markets, the awareness set for a particular product class may be as little as three or fewer brands, when there are more than 20 brands in the product class. In such markets, the marketer of the lesser-known brand must attempt to increase the intensity of awareness by developing a strong relationship between the brand and a limited number of variables.

Competing directly with dominant brands is not advised. Instead, the marketer must identify as a target a position within a market segment that is not dominated by a leading brand. Alternatively, the marketer must concentrate on a variable that is highly prized by a particular market segment.

### 5.5.2.5 Analyse the brand's current position

From the data collected from consumers about their perceptions of the various brands in the market, the marketer can establish how strongly a particular brand is associated with a variety of determinant variables. To do this, a positioning map, similar to the one shown in Figure 5.5, is developed. Brands that are close to each other on the map can be expected to be close rivals, while those that are far apart on the map are considered very different from each other. Competitive rivalry between such brands is expected to be limited.

### 5.5.2.6 Determine customers' most preferred combination of attributes

The discussion so far has focused on consumers' perceptions of existing brands and has not given any insight into the positions that would appeal most to consumers. This can be achieved by asking survey respondents to think of the ideal product or brand within a particular product category. Respondents would be asked to rate their ideal product and existing products on a number of determinant variables. The result of such an analysis of South African airlines in the mid-1990s is shown in Figure 5.7. The determinant variables that are closest to the ideal point are more important to consumers, while those that are further apart from each other are considered less important.

FIGURE 5.7    PERCEPTUAL MAP OF SOUTH AFRICAN AIRLINES BASED ON IDEAL POINTS

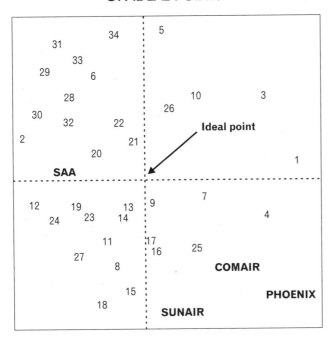

**Attributes associated**
1. Best/reasonable prices
2. Most expensive prices
3. Good value for money
4. Good/special offers/discount
5. Convenient flight times
6. Frequent flights
7. Good safety records/safe
8. Modern aeroplanes
9. Well maintained aircraft
10. Punctual/arrive on time
11. Efficient, reliable reservations
12. 24 hours reservation system
13. Fast, efficient check-in system
14. Efficient luggage handling system
15. Friendly/helpful ground staff
16. Friendly/helpful cabin crew
17. Personal service/feel special
18. Neat, presentable cabin crew
19. Informative crew
20. Crew acknowledge FF
21. Confortable/relaxed flights
22. Good food on flights
23. Hot meals
24. Free drinks
25. Real crockery and cutlery
26. Legroom between seats
27. Good incentive packages FF
28. Lounge facility access FF
29. Priority waiting list FF
30. Special gifts for FF
31. Access to year up-grade FF
32. Additional baggage FF
33. Separate check-in FF
34. Rapid check-in FF
(FF - Frequent flyer)

Attribute positions are approximate

Source: Adapted from Louw, NS. 1996. An integrated marketing approach for a medium-sized South African airline in a deregulated market. Unpublished MCom dissertation. Rand Afrikaans University, p 242.

## 5.5.2.7 Select positioning strategies

Deciding where to position a new brand or where to reposition an existing one depends on the market targeting analysis discussed earlier, as well as the market positioning analysis. The position chosen must reflect customer preferences and the positions of competitive brands. The decision must also reflect the expected future attractiveness of the target market and the relative strengths and weaknesses of competitors as well as the organisation's own capabilities. Specific positioning methods are discussed in paragraph 5.5.3.

## 5.5.3 Positioning methods

In general, seven positioning methods can be distinguished[12]:

1. ***Attribute positioning***

   The enterprise positions itself in terms of one or more outstanding attributes. Benson & Hedges has chosen to position its cigarettes in terms of lightness and taste.

2. ***Benefit positioning***

   This positioning method emphasises the unique benefits that the enterprise or product offering offers its customers. For example, Gillette Contour blades promise a closer shave.

3. ***Use/application positioning***

   An enterprise can position itself or its products in terms of the product use or application possibility. Graça wine, for example, is positioned as a wine to be enjoyed at all kinds of fun occasions.

4. ***User positioning***

   The enterprise may position their products with their users in mind. Marketers of bungee jumping can position their market offering to appeal to the thrill-seekers.

5. ***Competitor positioning***

   Some products can best be positioned against competitive offerings. BMW finds it useful to position their cars directly against that of Mercedes-Benz, their closest rival in South Africa.

6. ***Product category positioning***

   An enterprise can position itself in a product category not traditionally associated with it, thereby expanding business opportunities. A museum or planetarium, traditionally regarded as an educational institution, may elect to position itself as a tourist attraction.

## 7. *Quality/price positioning*

The enterprise may claim their product is of exceptional quality, or the lowest price. While Edgars is known for high quality garments, Pep Stores is known for unbeatable prices.

After the marketer has decided on a particular positioning method, it must be communicated to the target market. Sun International has chosen to position its resorts as superior in quality. They employ all elements of the marketing strategy to communicate this quality image:

- The product itself reflects the positioning method to be used. Close inspection of the facilities, decor and ambience of the Lost City will confirm this.

- Price can be a strong indicator of quality, and the prices at Sun International reflect this.

- The efficiency of the distribution system (or Central Reservation System) can enhance the quality perception even further.

- The communication material about Sun International resorts reflect quality in the form of expensive paper, excellent photographs and layout (brochures), professional radio adverts and spectacular television advertisements.

## SUMMARY

Market segmentation remains one of the cornerstones of modern marketing. In this chapter, we defined the main theoretical concepts associated with market segmentation, targeting and positioning, and explained how it can be applied by marketers. It is imperative for marketing management to realise that they cannot hope to satisfy all markets. Instead, they must divide the heterogeneous market into more homogeneous groups of customers; choose one or more to target with their product offering(s); and position themselves relative to their competitors. Ultimately, the success of marketing management will depend on their ability to select profitable target markets in an ever-changing marketing environment, as well as their ability to satisfy the needs of the chosen segment(s).

# REFERENCES

1. Kotler, P. 1997. *Marketing management: analysis, planning, implementation and control.* Englewood Cliffs, NJ: Prentice Hall, pp 268-269.

2. Macintosh, RW and Goeldner, CR 1990. *Tourism: principles, practices, philosophies.* New York: John Wiley & Son, p 377.

3. Kotler *op cit* p 258.

4. South African Advertising research Foundation. 1993. The South African Advertising Research Foundation's living standards measure (LSM). November.

5. Assael, H. 1993. *Marketing: principles and strategy.* Fort Worth: Dryden Press, p 320.

6. Walker, OC; Boyd, HW and Larréché, JC. 1996. *Marketing strategy: planning and implementation.* Chicago: Richard D Irwin, p 156.

7. Berkowitz, EN; Kerin, RA; Hartley, SW and Rudelius, W. 1994. *Marketing.* Burr Ridge, Ill: Richard D Irwin, pp 244 – 245.

8. Walker, Boyd & Larréché *op cit* p 162.

9. Lewinson, DM. 1996. *Marketing management: an overview.* Fort Worth: Dryden, p. 213.

10. Kotler *op cit* p 283.

11. Walker, Boyd and Larréché *op cit* p 182.

12. Kotler *op cit* pp 299 – 300.

CHAPTER **6**

# INTEGRATED MARKETING

## 6.1 INTRODUCTION

The previous five chapters have established the core analysis and information sources that need to be identified, researched and discussed before any marketing decisions can be made. These core information areas form the basis for designing an informed and effective market offering. There is a strong tendency to discuss solutions or to prepare answers before the problem has been identified! In this chapter, we establish how each of the previous chapters affect the decisions made by marketers in terms of offering a product or service to the marketplace. We will now establish the link between these core information areas and the market decisions.

### LEARNING OUTCOMES

After you have studied this chapter you will be able to:

- explain how the marketing concept relates to the critical marketing decisions;

- explain how marketing information can be obtained through the MIS;

- explain the effect of the environment on the design of the marketing mix;

- discuss how the determinants of consumer behaviour influence marketing decision making; and

- identify how the choice of target market determines the design of the market offering

## 6.2 THE MARKETING PROCESS

Van der Walt *et al*[1] explain that there are four major areas about which marketing management must make decisions. Once the target market is chosen, the marketer must make decisions about what to offer (*the product*), the place where the product is to be sold or delivered to the customer (*distribution of the product*), how the customer will be informed about the product (*marketing communications*), and the *price* of the product, which should reflect the value of the product to the customer. The four variables combine to represent the *market offering* which the marketer develops in order to meet and satisfy the needs of the customer. These four variables (also known as the four Ps) are known as the marketing mix.

Figure 6.1 shows how the core analysis and topics discussed in the previous chapters interact in the marketing process in order to facilitate the achievement of the enterprise's objectives. Once the target market is chosen and its needs properly understood through research, the marketing mix can be developed in order to meet the market needs. If this is done successfully, the marketer can contribute to the main objective of any business, namely the maximisation of profitability in the long term. This occurs within the context of a dynamic marketing environment.

Some authors[2] have questioned whether the traditional marketing mix (the four Ps) is an adequate mix for marketing of service products. They have proposed an expanded mix, which is more comprehensive and would also cover service products. The three elements added to the traditional mix to form this expanded mix are:

1. *Customer service* – this helps marketing management to differentiate The business and helps to build closer relationships with customers.

2. *People* – the staff form an integral part of the product, especially those employees who are involved in high levels of contact with customers.

3. *Processes* – the policies and procedures of the business influence how a product or service is created or delivered to customers.

Let us now examine each of the main components (and chapters) of this book and their relation to the marketing mix.

## FIGURE 6.1 THE MARKETING PROCESS

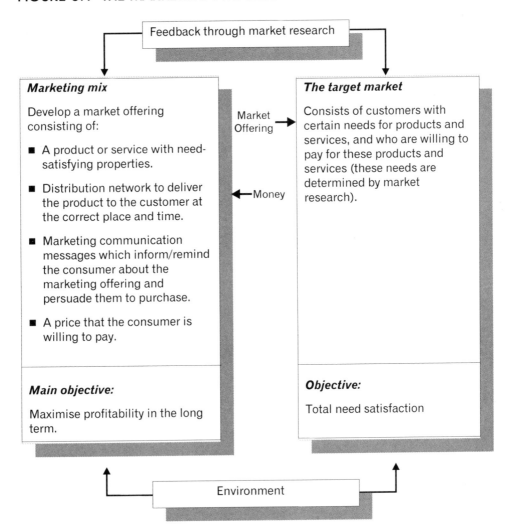

Source: Adapted from Van der Walt, *et al*. 1996. *Marketing management*. 3rd ed. Cape Town: Juta, p 11.

## 6.3 MARKET ORIENTATION

A business that has a marketing orientation has three important characteristics[3].

1. **Customer focus** – the striving to discover customer needs so that satisfaction can be delivered.

2. **A team approach** – using cross-functional teams and an integrated approach to develop and deliver customer solutions.

3. **Competitor orientation** –  a continuous recognition of where competitors have an advantage, their competitive position and marketing strategies

These three key characteristics lead to a business being in a position to deliver satisfaction to its customers. If this is measured, and if the business performs in delivering satisfaction to the customer effectively, the profitability of the business can be enhanced through better customer retention and increased loyalty. This is evidenced by the following benefits that a loyal customer can ensure for a business over a period of time:

■ increased purchases;

■ reduced operating costs;

■ referrals to other potential customers; and

■ the ability to justify a price premium to differentiate the product from price competitors.

When this marketing orientation is coupled to effectiveness in the marketplace, the profitability of the business is reinforced. Figure 6.2 shows this relationship.

## FIGURE 6.2  DRIVERS OF BUSINESS PROFITABILITY

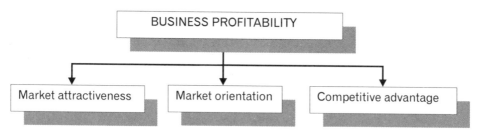

Source: Adapted from Best, RJ. 1997. *Market-based management.* Upper Saddle River: Prentice Hall, p 8.

Best[4] summarises the effect of a strong marketing orientation by stating that the ultimate goal of a strong marketing orientation is to develop and implement marketing strategies that attract, satisfy and retain target market customers! This is done through the marketing strategy, which includes the target market and the marketing mix, as shown in Figure 6.3.

## FIGURE 6.3  MARKETING ORIENTATION SHAPES MARKETING DECISIONS

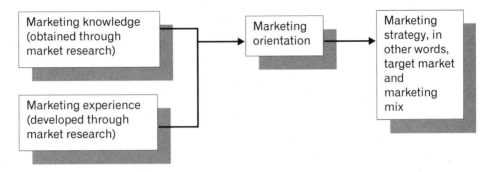

Source: Adapted from Best, RJ. 1997. *Market-based management.* Upper Saddle River: Prentice Hall, p 25.

### ENVIRONMENTAL CHANGE AND MARKETING MIX ADAPTION

In 1982, the United States company Morton International acquired a company that had automobile airbags in its product portfolio. They were considered difficult to manufacture and were positively disliked by the prime customer group, the car manufacturers. Morton anticipated that in time airbags would become a standard feature in all cars sold in the United States and elsewhere. The company invested heavily in improving airbag quality and reducing production costs. In 1995, there was a law passed in the United States that legislated the fitment of airbags in all vehicles sold in the USA. Morton achieved a 55% share of the world market for airbags with excellent prospects for growth.

Source: Adapted from Ennew, C. 1993. *The marketing blueprint.* Oxford: Blackwell, p 52.

## 6.4 THE MARKETING ENVIRONMENT

In Chapter 2 you learned that the marketing environment of a company is dynamic and made up of a number of sub-environments. What is important to remember is that the environment consists of a number of interacting influences. There are uncontrollable variables, such as those that comprise the macro environment (economic, political, social and technological).

These can be contrasted with those variables under the direct control of marketing. The marketing mix, for example, is under the direct control of marketing management.

Marketing managers need to understand the wider business environment (macro environment), but they should concentrate on those aspects which can be influenced, such as the controllable variables of product, price, communication and distribution. Adcock *et al*[5] point out that it is necessary to stress that the controllable variables are indirectly affected by these uncontrollable elements in the environment. The marketer must ensure that those variables that can be controlled reflect the realities of the uncontrollable variables in the marketing environment. This is illustrated in Figure 6.4.

## FIGURE 6.4 ENVIRONMENTAL INFLUENCE

| Company | | Marketing environment |
|---|---|---|
| Marketing activities and plans (controllables) | Major direction of influence | (Uncontrollable variables in the macro environment) |
| ■ product | ← | ■ economic |
| ■ price | | ■ social |
| ■ communication | | ■ technological |
| ■ distribution | | ■ political |

Source: Adcock, D et al. 1993. *Marketing principles and practice*. London: Pitman, p 24.

The effectiveness of marketing will be determined by how well it can match the business's offerings to the requirements from the marketplace. Marketers will need to develop an outside-in orientation. This will be seen in the ability of the company to respond to changes in the environment, and is in effect the strategic role of the marketing function in the organisation.

This is not an easy task, as evidenced by the many organisations that have disappeared or have lost market share to competitors. Many businesses become preoccupied with these daily operational problems (often termed fire-fighting) and tend to lose contact with the environment, often ignoring or discounting the small changes that are the precursors to more serious change.

Figure 6.5 illustrates a framework for environmental monitoring and adaption. The environmental monitoring identifies short-run changes or long-term trends. These are translated into opportunities, threats or inconsequential events. If adaptation is required, it must be reflected in the controllable aspects of the marketing mix. In other words, the business must change something to respond to the change!

## FIGURE 6.5 ENVIRONMENTAL ADAPTATION AND MONITORING

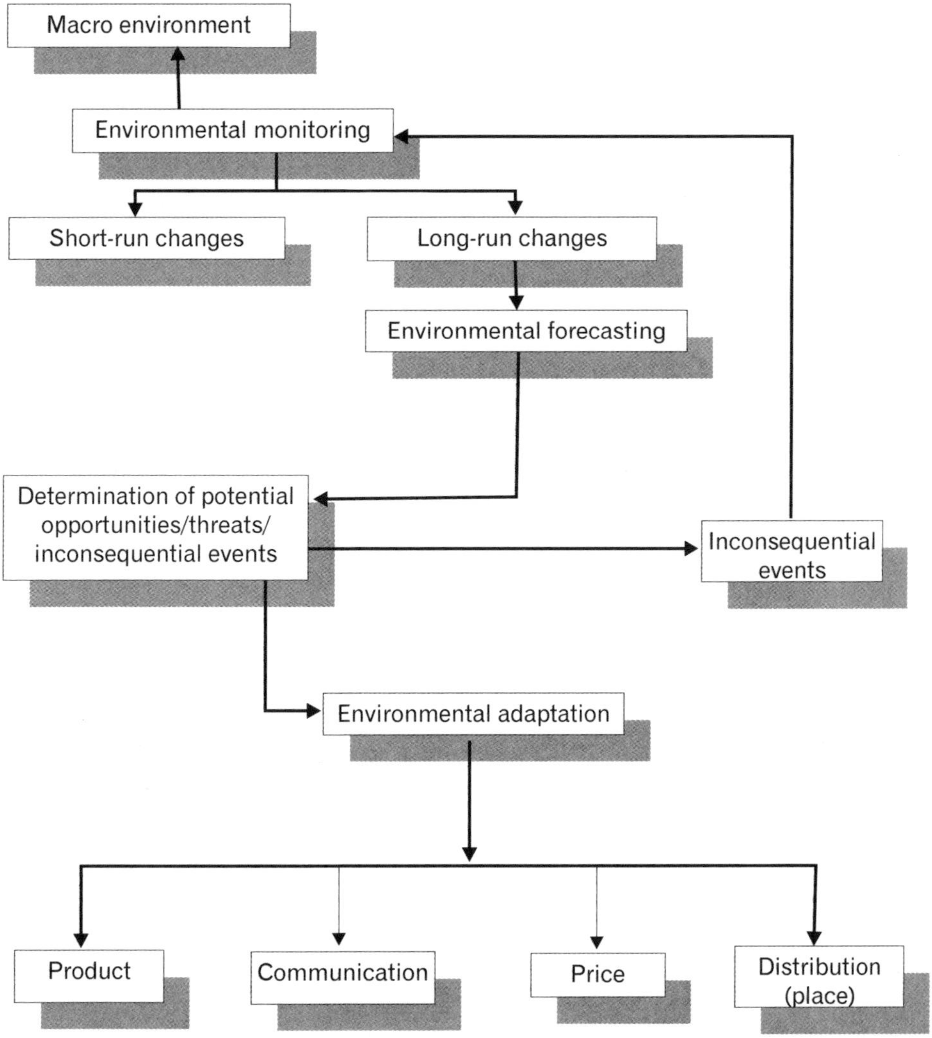

```
Macro environment
        ↑
Environmental monitoring ←─────────────────────┐
        │                                       │
   ┌────┴──────┐                                │
   ↓           ↓                                │
Short-run   Long-run changes                    │
changes         │                               │
                ↓                               │
        Environmental forecasting               │
                │                               │
Determination of potential ←────┘               │
opportunities/threats/ ─────────→ Inconsequential
inconsequential events             events
        │
        ↓
Environmental adaptation
        │
   ┌────┬────────┬────────┬────────┐
   ↓    ↓        ↓        ↓
Product Communication Price Distribution
                              (place)
```

Source: Adapted from Busch, PS & Houston, MJ. 1985. *Marketing: strategic foundations.* Homewood: Irwin, p 82.

## EXAMPLES OF RESPONDING TO ENVIRONMENTAL CHANGE

- Signorelli Outfitters, a small tailoring and outfitting business, had to relocate their premises out of the Pretoria central business district to a suburban mall in order to respond the changing clothes shopping habits of its customers.

- The City Lodge concept was borne out of the changing needs and requirements of the South African consumer for cheaper, value-for-money accommodation.

- Toyota SA responded to the changing competitive structure of the after-sales marketing environment by initiating a Welcome to Our World After-Sales Service Programme and a 'Book-of-Life' advertising and promotional campaign.

Source: Adapted from Cant, M and Machado, R (eds). 1998. *Marketing success stories*. Pretoria: International Thompson Publishing.

## 6.5   OBTAINING AND USING MARKETING INFORMATION

The contents of Chapter 3 should have convinced you that it is imperative for a marketing organisation to have an effective marketing information system (MIS). The marketing information system helps to integrate all the different types of marketing information and makes this information available to the decision makers in a useful and timely form. This is illustrated in figure 6.6.

### FIGURE 6.6   SOURCES OF INFORMATION

Source: Adapted from Hutt, RW and Stull, WA. 1992. *Marketing: an introduction*. Cincinnati: South-Western, p 96.

The purpose of the MIS is to collect, analyse and evaluate all the information that is likely to be of value when making marketing and other decisions[6]. This means that the information system is situated between the marketers making decisions and the marketing environment. It is, in effect, the interface between the two. Note that it is not just marketing that makes use of the information. Production operations, research and development and all the other functions in the business should have access to this information. The MIS will also help the company to attempt to identify possible change and react to the change, as discussed in the previous section. Many companies have formal MIS structures, yet some small businesses do not have a formal system and are very effective using their informal channels to keep in touch with the market.

## FIGURE 6.7 MIS AND MARKETING DECISION MAKING

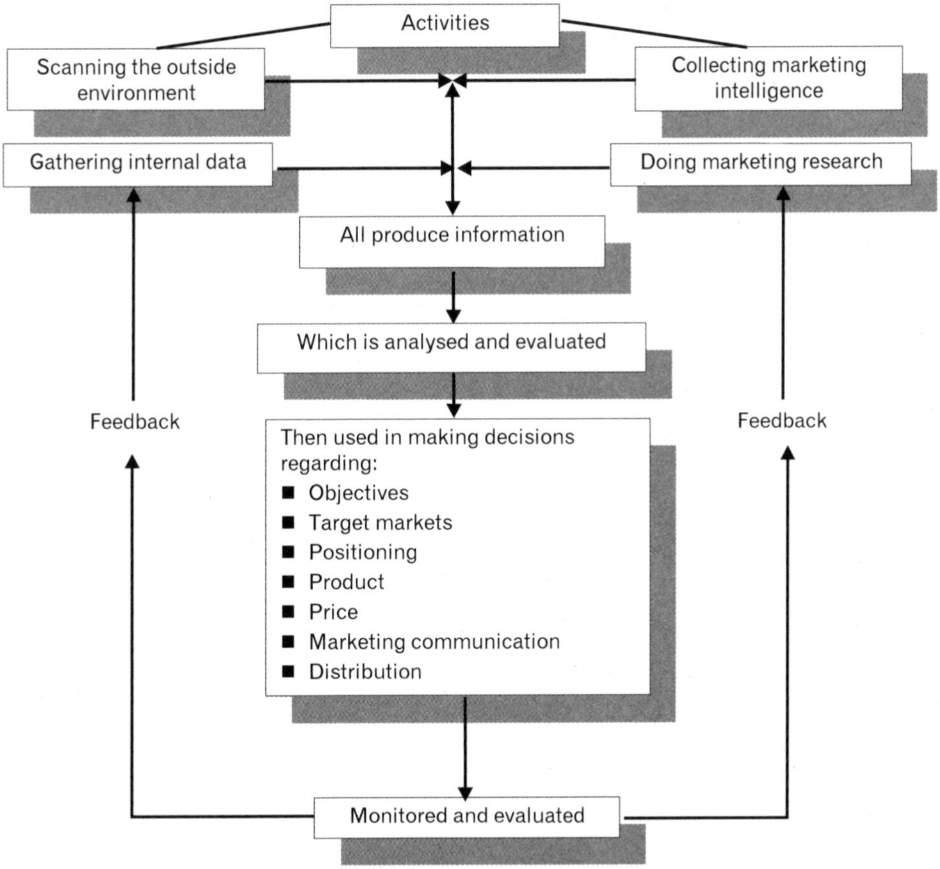

Source: Adapted from Anderson, AH and Dobson, T. 1994. *Effective marketing.* Oxford: Blackwell, p 77.

Figure 6.7 shows the connection between the information received and marketing decisions. The figure indicates the firm's activities in terms of gathering data and information. Once this information has been analysed and evaluated, marketing management must respond to the information received by making key marketing decisions, as indicated. These changes or responses to the environment are then monitored and evaluated to determine whether the organisation is aligned to the environment and to the market. Remember, the value of information is in its use, so decisions must be made as to how to respond to meaningful change in the marketing environment!

## 6.6 PERSPECTIVES ON CONSUMER BEHAVIOUR

One of the basic premises of marketing is that by understanding customers and their purchasing habits, marketers can design an effective offering to help them achieve their objectives.

There are many basic questions that any marketer must be able to answer about the market, such as who the customers are and why they buy. This information is invaluable because marketing is supposed to be the link between the customers and the organisation. Figure 6.8 illustrates the relationship between the environment, the marketer and the customer.

## FIGURE 6.8 A SIMPLE MODEL OF BUYER BEHAVIOUR

| EXTERNAL STIMULI | | THE BUYER | | THE BUSINESS DECISIONS |
|---|---|---|---|---|
| Environ-mental factors | Marketing mix factors | Buyer character-istics | Buyer decision process | Choice of: ■ product ■ brand ■ dealer ■ quantity ■ timing |
| ■ Economic ■ Social ■ Political ■ Technical | ■ Product ■ Price ■ Marketing communication ■ Distribution | | | |

INPUTS - - - - - - - - - - - - - - - - - - - - - - - - - - - - - - ▶ OUTPUTS

Source: Adapted from Wilson, RMS and Gilligan, C. 1997. *Strategic marketing management.* Oxford: Butterworth-Heineman, p 157.

You will notice from Figure 6.8 that the environmental variables under which all market players operate have an influence on the customer. Likewise, the marketing mix designed by the marketer should also have an effect on the customer. These two aspects are **external stimuli** to the customer. There are also internal stimuli which affect the decisions made by the customer. The buyer's own characteristics, for example, will effect his/her decisions. Different customers will have different perceptions and expectations, and the manner in which the buyer proceeds through the decision-making process will also affect the customer's decision. Each customer may have different individual or group influences, and no two customers are exactly alike. The involvement of the buyer with the product will help to determine how seriously and systematically he/she proceeds through the steps in the decision-making process. Lastly, the buyer will make a number of decisions. The marketer's job, through the marketing mix, is to persuade the buyer to buy the marketer's products, and to deliver the need satisfaction to ensure that the buyer will remain a loyal customer.

As previously mentioned, the marketing environment is constantly changing, and must be monitored in order for the business to respond to changes in the marketing environment. Likewise, the customers are also affected by changes in the environment, and their needs will also change. Any business, in order to be successful, must be aware of changing characteristics and needs of its customer base. These could be significant changes, which the business will have to address through its marketing activities.

Wilson and Gilligan[7] have identified a number of characteristics which are associated with what they term the 'new' consumer:

- the development of new value systems;

- greater emphasis on value for money;

- higher levels of price awareness and price sensitivity;

- an increased demand for and a willingness to accept more and exciting new products;

- less fear of technology;

- lower levels of brand and supplier loyalty;

- greater willingness to experiment with new products, ideas and delivery systems;

- a greater cynicism;

- higher levels of environmental awareness;

- greater scepticism about politicians, big business and traditional institutions; and

- the changing roles of men and women.

The connection of these characteristics with the marketing mix are self-evident.

The core of any marketing strategy is a commitment to understanding customer needs and problems. Figure 6.9 depicts this customer analysis.

## FIGURE 6.9  CUSTOMER ANALYSIS AND THE MARKETING MIX

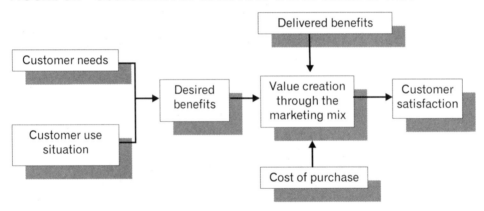

Source: Adapted from Best, RJ. 1997. *Market-based management.* Upper Saddle River: Prentice Hall, p 110.

In Figure 6.9, we see that a business must monitor the changing customer needs and the changing ways in which the customer uses the product. These two factors will affect the benefits which the customer is seeking and which the customer desires. The business responds to these through changes in some aspect of the marketing mix. By successfully meeting these customer needs and delivering the benefits desired, the business can satisfy its customers, increasing the likelihood of success. Note that the customers determine what value they receive from a business by considering the benefits which they perceive as being delivered to them against the cost of the product/service. This emphasises the importance of marketing management ensuring that its customers' perceive that they are receiving value-for-money relative to what they would receive from competitors.

## 6.7 TARGET MARKET SELECTION AND POSITIONING

The importance of target market selection and positioning is best understood in terms of the phenomenon of ***fragmentation***[8], whereby technology and cultural differences contribute to the splintering of the market into diverse groups. These are environmental aspects, many of which work together. In selecting a target market, marketers need to understand how to recognise the various groups which make up the total market. This process relies on marketing research which assists the marketer to find the best way to segment the market.

After the different segments have been identified, the market potential of each segment must be established. Again, market research is instrumental in the selection of segments that will help the company to achieve its objectives.

Having decided on a specific target market(s), the marketer will have to determine how to position the product in the target market. In order to do this, further market research in terms of the competitor positions and need satisfaction may be required. Chapter 5 discussed the different options for positioning a product. Once the positioning strategy has been established, the marketing mix must be tailored to meet customer needs effectively. The marketing mix, if correctly designed, is the method by which the marketer meets the needs of the customers in such a way that the customer's perception of the product matches the positioning strategy selected by the marketer.

Note that there are continuous changes in the market, so the environment must be monitored continuously to determine whether repositioning is needed or not. Figure 6.10 shows the progression in terms of segmenting, targeting, positioning, and designing the marketing mix. Let us now consider the marketing mix itself.

FIGURE 6.10     PROGRESSION FOR PINPOINTING THE MARKET

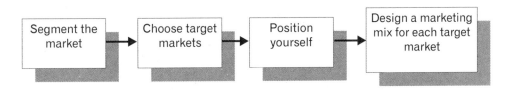

Source: Adapted from Machado, R. 1996. *Marketing for a small business*. Cape Town: Juta, p 51.

## 6.8 THE MARKETING MIX

The previous seven sections of this chapter formed the basis for this book. These are the building blocks upon which an effective marketing campaign is based. The care and attention to detail exercised by the marketer with these building blocks will help him/her in terms of the key decision-making areas of marketing. These key decision-making areas are the choice of a target market/s and the design of an appropriate marketing mix for the chosen target market/s. The choice of a target market and positioning of the product offering in that target market were dealt with in chapter 5 and briefly in paragraph 6.7.

The second key decision-making area is the marketing mix. Although it is not the aim of this book to discuss the marketing mix in detail, we do need to introduce what the marketing mix is and briefly discuss the impact of these building blocks on the components of the marketing mix.

The marketing mix is a combination of marketing decisions designed to influence customers to buy the enterprise's products and/or services[9]. A more common term used to describe this mix is the '**Four Ps**' of marketing: product, promotion, place and price. The **product** aspect of the marketing mix tries to ensure that the product characteristics match the benefits sought by the target customers. The **promotion** element tries to communicate the enterprise's ability to satisfy the customer through the use of communication such as advertising, personal selling, sales promotions and publicity.

The **place** or distribution component of the marketing mix tries to deliver the right product to the right place at the right time to satisfy customer needs. Lastly, the price component of the mix tries to match the money that customers will pay for the product with the value customers receive through the purchase and use of the product. These four components work together to help the enterprise to achieve its marketing objectives, as shown in Figure 6.11 and briefly discussed below.

### FIGURE 6.11 THE FOUR Ps OF MARKETING

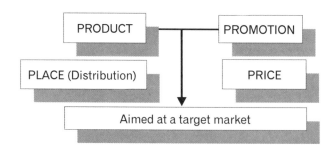

## 6.8.1 Product decisions

Product decisions are critical. The marketer must determine what the actual product offers, as well as the need-satisfying benefits which should be included. The marketer needs to make decisions regarding the range of different types of products and/or services to make and offer. This is called the **product mix**.

### HARLEY DAVIDSON MOTORCYCLES AND THE FOUR Ps

Harley Davidson used the four Ps of marketing to position its motorcycles to a new customer segment: the baby boomer generation in the United States. The product was changed by introducing a new engine, but the heavy metal look was retained. The promotional strategy was changed by shifting the advertising to promote a softer image. It featured celebrities, such as actress Elizabeth Taylor, on a Harley Davidson. The objective was to attract the high-income segment. It changed its distribution strategy by cleaning up the dealerships so that they did not look so dark and so that they were more customer-friendly. Harley Davidson do not only sell motorcycles now but also motorcycle fashion accessories which are displayed in a clean, bright atmosphere. They price their motorcycles to reflect the value that the high-income earners place on living out their fantasies on a Harley Davidson motorcycle. The upper end of the motorcycle range often runs into the $20 000 price range. All these components demonstrate a well-co-ordinated marketing mix targeted to a specific segment of the market.

Source: Adapted from Assael, H. 1998. *Marketing*. Orlando: The Dryden Press, pp 18-19.

Specific product strategies must be established: Whether the product mix will be extended through product diversification; whether it will be reduced for more specialisation; whether to standardise the product range; how to differentiate or distinguish the product from other competitive products; and decisions on how to manage the possible obsolescence of the product. A plan for the development and commercialisation of the products must be developed. The product design and package design are important, as they are so closely related to product decisions. The whole issue of a brand name and the branding decisions must be addressed, and plans made to establish a brand awareness within the selected target markets .

Although product is usually the first component of the marketing mix addressed by marketing, the development and design of the product offering and package is totally dependant on the input from the environmental analysis and customer analyses.  Without researching these two areas, the marketer cannot effectively design a product offering to meet the needs of the customer.  For example, changing economic conditions may necessitate developing a lower-priced product item.  Toyota SA developed the Tazz range of motorcars as a response to economic changes in the marketplace that generated more attention on entry-level motorcar offerings.  Evolving use of products may necessitate packaging design changes.  Both of these could lead to new product opportunities and/or brand extensions.

## 6.8.2 Pricing decisions

Price is important because it is the only element in the marketing mix that generates the revenue. It is also important because it affects the enterprise in a direct way, namely the profitability of the business. The marketer will need to establish the price sensitivity of the target customers, and will then need to establish the basic price. This can be done on the basis of costs, on the basis of the demand for a product, or on the basis of competitive pricing structures. All three of these factors will influence the setting of a price. The marketer must also establish flexibility in the pricing structure through the use of adjustments. These factors could include different types of discounts and the geographic location of the customers.

We have referred to the effect of the enviroment on pricing by noting that economic conditions could lead a marketer to develop a lower-priced alternative.  The marketer must monitor the environment to analyse the effect of the environmental factors on pricing.  New developments in materials and processes can have significant impact on a business's bottom line as a result of its impact in pricing and margins. Technology, in particular, has provided significant threats to many businesses by its accelerating rate of change, yet it also provides opportunities to improve bottom-line performance by improving profitability. Developments such as 'just-in-time', materials management systems, and e-commerce have had a significant impact on the profit margins of motorcar manufacturers.  Many cars are now sold by means of the Internet, with significant impact on promotion and distribution costs and therefore on pricing.  Marketers must also carefully research and monitor the traget market's sensitivity to its pricing strategy.  Marlboro is the leading cigarette brand in the world, yet it had to implement a significant price decrease a few years ago, when research revealed that it was losing market share because smokers were switching to lower-priced or generic cigarettes in response to the price of Marlboro which they perceived to be high. The price decrease, although shocking in terms of traditional marketing strategy, did succeed in regaining lost market share for Marlboro.

### 6.8.3 Distribution decisions

The marketer will have to establish the intensity of distribution needed to meet the market's needs and expectations. This could be *intensive*, *selective* or *exclusive* distribution intensity. The marketer will also have to decide on the type of distribution channel through which to deliver the product/service to the final consumers. There are many options to consider here, from direct channels through to those that utilise intermediaries such as retailers, wholesalers and agents. The effect of the physical position of the marketer's own business could be included here, as the location of a business is often the most critical determinant of possible success.

Distribution decisions and distribution channel design is one of the areas where rapid changes are occuring in terms of the marketing mix. The use of the Internet for direct sales is revolutionising the way many firms reach its customers. Dell computers recently overtook Compaq as the leading personal computer seller in the USA, and Dell has a completely different distribution strategy to Compaq. While Compaq distributes through the traditional computer retailer channels, Dell uses a direct channel by selling to customers by means of the Internet. This innovation has led to significant reductions in distribution costs and has also had a direct effect on its pricing policy. It is critical for marketers to monitor both changes in the environment and customer expectations of where they want to purchase products. In so doing, they will always be able to meet customer needs by providing the right product at the right time.

### 6.8.4 Promotion decisions

It is essential for marketers to inform current and potential customers in the marketplace about their products and their marketing activities. This communication can be done by using marketing communication tools such as advertising, sales promotion, personal selling and publicity.

It is clear that there are a number of decisions associated with the use of these communication tools, such as what message to deliver, what media to use, what size budget is required, and what promotional support activities to implement. All of these must be implemented, co-ordinated and evaluated. The marketer must also communicate internally throughout the organisation to ensure that the employees and staff are aware of what the expectations are in the marketplace and what message the organisation is delivering to its target audiences.

Media choices are an area to which marketers must pay particular attention. The growing number of media choices (Internet, intranet, hot-air balloons, travelling billboards, new magazines and new television stations such as satellite television and e-TV) means that marketers have to pay particular attention to making the correct choices for communicating with the target markets in an effective manner. This requires systematic research of the customer base to monitor trends in terms of media as well as advetising campaign impact. Nando's, for example, have been particularly affective in designing campaigns that are related in to current events in South Africa. Their success is as a result of monitoring the environment for opportunities.

## SUMMARY

In this chapter, we have established how the topics covered in the previous five chapters help to shape the decisions made by marketers in terms of the marketing mix. In fact, a number of analyses were needed in order to accomplish this. Firstly, the marketing orientation of the business was analysed to ensure that the company culture is correct and proactive. Secondly, the marketing environment and its effect in all the decision-making areas of marketing were highlighted. Thirdly, we emphasised the importance of marketing research in order to align the market offering with the marketing environment and to meet customer needs. This all entails a thorough understanding of the customer and the characteristics that affect the decisions made in terms of purchasing. Lastly, target market selection and positioning is critical, as all the decisions made by marketing are made as a result of selection and positioning. They are the main consideration for all marketing decisions. Figure 6.12 places the philosophy and approach discussed in this book into context.

## FIGURE 6.12  CORE ANALYSIS FOR MARKETING DECISIONS

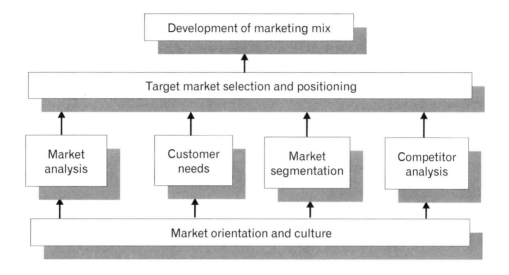

## REFERENCES

1. Van der Walt, A; Strydom, JW; Marx, S and Jooste, CJ. 1996. *Marketing management*. Cape Town: Juta, pp 8 – 12.

2. McDonald, MS and Payne, A. 1996. *Marketing planning for services*. Oxford: Butterworth-Heineman, pp 18-20.

3. Best, RJ. 1997. *Market-based management*. Upper Saddle River: Prentice Hall, pp 8-11.

4. Best p 25.

5. Adcock, D; Bradfield, R; Helborg, A and Ross, C. 1993. *Marketing principles and practice*. London: Pitman, p 25.

6. Anderson, AH and Dobson, T. 1994. *Effective marketing*. Oxford: Blackwell, pp 76 – 78.

7. Wilson, RMS and Gilligan, C. 1997. *Strategic marketing management*. Oxford: Butterworth-Heineman, p 158.

8. Solomon, MR and Stuart, EW. 1997. *Marketing: real people, real choices*. Upper Saddle River: Prentice Hall, p 28.

9. Assael, H. 1998. *Marketing*. Orlando: The Dryden Press, pp 1.8-1.9.